James Fitz

Sweet Potato Culture

James Fitz

Sweet Potato Culture

ISBN/EAN: 9783337407094

Printed in Europe, USA, Canada, Australia, Japan

Cover: Foto ©Suzi / pixelio.de

More available books at **www.hansebooks.com**

SWEET POTATO CULTURE.

GIVING FULL INSTRUCTIONS FROM

Starting the Plants to Harvesting and Storing the Crop.

WITH A CHAPTER ON THE CHINESE YAM.

NEW AND ENLARGED EDITION.

BY

JAMES FITZ.

AUTHOR OF "SOUTHERN APPLE AND PEACH CULTURIST."

NEW YORK:

ORANGE JUDD COMPANY,

1903

CONTENTS.

(3)

PREFACE TO THE NEW AND GREATLY ENLARGED EDITION.

———◆◆◆———

The greatly increased demand for what we have already written on the sweet potato encourages us to use all the means of information within our reach, to add further value to this treatise. We have, through the courtesy of correspondents in the various sweet potato regions, elicited information and views on propagation and culture, which we endorse as eminently practical and useful, and which will doubtless render this work (the only one published on this subject) indispensable as a book of "quick and convenient reference" to all cultivators of the sweet potato.

It is not easy to estimate the value of the additional instruction and experience in the added chapters. All needed information, it is believed, is now given which can tend to render this increasing industry more profitable by means of intelligent culture.

The modes of culture and management suitable for different sections are somewhat various. This requires attention. For instance, the vines are allowed to take hold on the ridges and produce extra crops in some parts of the South, while in the Northern and Middle States this cannot be permitted without detriment to the crop. The length of the growing season makes this difference.

Having collected and arranged additional matter that must render our work more useful, we submit it to the public, hoping to merit the increased confidence and approval of all culturists.

THE AUTHOR.

Keswick, Va., September 1st, 1886.

(5)

PREFACE.

The requisites for the proper production and cultivation of the Sweet Potato are probably less understood than those of any other crop of like importance.

The author, residing in a locality where the Sweet Potato comes to perfection, and having a practical knowledge of its cultivation, storing, etc., feels that, in the absence of any treatise on the subject, he may be able to supply a want in horticultural literature.

Whoever aids in increasing the supply of food, must be regarded as a public benefactor, and the author hopes that the instructions contained in this little work may promote the public welfare.

The author trusts that his friends in the Sweet Potato districts will not regard him as officious if he urges the importance of their looking to foreign markets for the disposal of their crops of the Sweet Potato. Now that steamships are constructed for the safe transportation of perishable articles, there would appear to be no reason why the Sweet Potato should not be a regular article of export, and it only needs coöperation between ship-owners and growers to secure this end.

CHAPTER I.

THE SWEET POTATO.—(*Ipomœa Batatas*, Lam.)

The Sweet Potato belongs to the Convolvulus or Morning-Glory Family, (the *Convolvulaceæ*), and in the various revisions of this large and somewhat difficult family, the Sweet Potato has been assigned to several different genera. Hence we find it in some works given as *Convolvulus Batatas*, of Linnæus; *C. esculentus*, and *C. tuberosus*, of other botanists. Choisy gives it as *Batatas edulis;* while the latest revision of the family, by Bentham and Hooker, in *Genera Plantarum*, places it under *Ipomœa*, hence, according to accepted botanical authority, the proper botanical name of the Sweet Potato is: *Ipomœa Batatas*, of Lamarck.

The native country of the Sweet Potato, as with many others of our cultivated plants, is still very doubtful. There is very strong evidence in favor of both its East Indian and American origin, but as the plant has not yet been found growing wild in either country, the question remains undecided.

That the potato mentioned by Shakespeare and contemporary writers, was this, and not the "White," or "Irish" potato, there seems to be little doubt.

The Sweet Potato is a perennial, with large, tuberous roots, and creeping stems; the leaves are very variable in shape, being heart-shaped, or halberd-shaped, with the lobes projecting, and it is not rare to find the leaves deeply lobed. The flower of the Sweet Potato is, in shape, like that of the common "Morning Glory," though not quite so spreading; it is of a purplish color in the throat, and white on the margin. The plant rarely produces flowers in the Northern States, but in the far South,

7

where the season is longer, flowers and ripened seeds are
not rare. The plant, as it runs along the ground, strikes
root at every joint, or node; this peculiarity, while advantageous in the far South, where the season is long
enough for such roots to grow to a useful size, are a dis-
advantage to the Northern cultivator, who lives where
the season is barely long enough for the principal roots to
mature.

VARIETIES OF THE SWEET POTATO.

As with other esculent vegetables, there are many
varieties of the Sweet Potato; these possess widely different qualities, which adapt them to the various soils and
climates of the several sections of the country. Which
particular variety will be best suited to a given locality,
can only be ascertained by experimental culture.

THE HANOVER SWEET POTATO, OR NANSEMOND IM-
PROVED.—The superiority of the Hanover variety may
be in part attributed to the congenial soil and climate of
the lower section of Virginia. The area more especially
adapted to the perfection of the Sweet Potato, Hanover
County, is limited, yet sufficiently extensive to supply
the Richmond market, and a large surplus for shipping.
The soil is a grayish, sandy loam, and has a clay subsoil, varying from a foot to many feet in depth. The
fine and almost impalpable sand, which covers most of its
surface, was deposited by the waters of the ocean ; this,
together with other sources of fertility, make up the
finely pulverized soil of Hanover, a locality that supplies
the markets of Richmond and other cities with various
vegetable productions. What are the elementary constituents of this soil is not known, and we have no reliable
analysis. "Nature seems to have made this locality
especially for a garden ; here the Sweet Potato and the
Melon find their own home." In regard to the Sweet

Potato the Editor of the "Southern Planter and Farmer" once said : "We may urge what we please, in connection with the Hanover Sweet Potato, and still not be deemed extravagant by any one at all acquainted with the excellence of this glorious tuber." An intelligent correspondent of "The American Farmer," Baltimore, says . "For our main crop of Sweet Potatoes for table use, we prefer the old 'Yellow Sweet' of Maryland and Virginia, called Yellow Nansemond at the North, known in the lower counties of the Eastern Shore, and the maritime counties of Virginia, and further south, almost exclusively by that name."

The Spanish Potato.—In tide-water Virginia, particularly on the eastern shore of both Maryland and Virginia, every farmer grows, besides the main crop, a few "Spanish Potatoes" for home use, though they are not usually eaten until the depth of winter, when they become "fat," as it is termed. Those who have never eaten a "fat" Spanish potato, do not yet know the capabilities of the Sweet Potato. But the "Spanish" is not productive, and it requires deeper soil and better culture for its long, ginger-like roots, and is seldom grown for market. This correspondent also says, in regard to

"The Southern Queen": "It is the earliest of all Sweet Potatoes. It was introduced some years ago from South America. It is in eating condition here, near Baltimore, usually by the middle of July, and when first dug is generally in good eating condition. As the season progresses, and during the fall and early winter, they are generally too wet to suit Southern palates ; while during this time the Yellow potatoes are in their glory. It is for keeping qualities that the 'Southern Queen' stands unrivalled. As a variety to begin and prolong the Sweet Potato season, there is nothing to compare with the 'Southern Queen.' The root is very large,

and much longer than that of the Nansemond ; is of a
very light color, and is said to be unrivalled as to keeping
qualities.   The vine is a vigorous grower, and the leaves
are larger and darker colored than those of the Nansemond.   Wherever it has been tried, a high estimate has
been placed upon its productiveness and good quality."
The leaves are not only larger, but they differ in shape
from those of the more common varieties. The engraving,

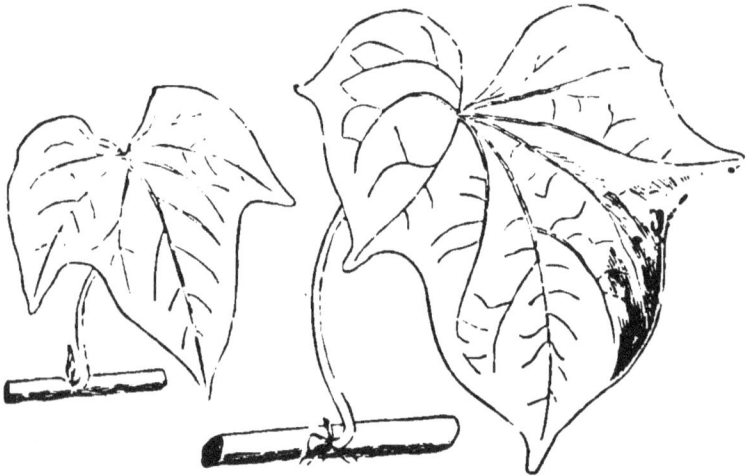

Fig. 1.   Fig. 2.

figure 1, gives a leaf of the Nansemond, and figure 2 one
of the Southern Queen, both reduced in the same proportion.

THE NANSEMOND. — Next to the "Hanover," or
"Nansemond Improved," this potato is in highest repute
in Northern markets, where it is called the Yellow Nansemond.   It takes its name from the south-eastern
county of Virginia, where it is said to have originated.
This, and other kinds, when propagated at the North,
are less sweet and less highly flavored than those produced in a warmer climate.   The New Jersey and Delaware Sweet Potatoes, which are marketed in New England, though palatable and largely consumed, and bring

good prices, are decidedly inferior to those raised in Virginia. We are informed that excellent Sweet Potatoes are raised in Southern Illinois, latitude 37°—38°, while those produced in Central Illinois, latitude 40°, are "watery," and comparatively insipid.

THE ROYAL SWEET POTATO OF HANOVER.—The Editor of the "Southern Planter and Farmer," Richmond, Va., says, in regard to this variety : "It was our good fortune to especially examine these magnificent Sweet Potatoes, exhibited at the State Fair by Mr. A. Tinsley, of Hanover, and others. We doubt if anything so fine as these potatoes has ever been seen before in this State; we certainly never have seen anything like them ; and in this judgment Col. B. Johnson Barber, and others, fully agreed with us. And to think of two hundred and forty-five bushels to the acre !" This "Royal Sweet Potato," we suppose, is identical with the Hanover Improved, or the Nansemond. It is not uncommon to find the same variety of fruits or vegetables in different sections under distinct names, and the writer has been quite recently reminded of this in the case of Sweet Potatoes.

THE YAM FAMILY OF SWEET POTATOES.—These consist of the "White" and "Yellow Bermuda," the "White California," and others. The roots are short and heavy, with red or white skin. They grow very large, especially in light, sandy soils. The "White Yam," and "Yellow Spanish," are, in the South, considered the most luscious and excellent of all potatoes for home use, though their exportation is limited.

A Western farmer, who claims to have extensive experience in the cultivation of Sweet Potatoes, gives his judgment concerning some of the leading varieties, as follows :

"The 'Yellow Pimento' has given the best satisfaction, in every respect, of any kinds we have tried. It is very productive, and of excellent quality, yielding always about double that others do. The 'Yellow Pimento' is also a good keeper and a good sprouter.

"The 'White Brazilian' is a very good potato, although the quality is not quite so good as that of the Pimento. This is the largest variety I grow, specimens often weighing from four to seven pounds. This is a shy sprouter, and hard to keep over winter.

"'Red Bermuda' is very productive, early, a good sprouter, and keeps well, but is of rather inferior quality.

"'White Bermuda' is not quite so productive as the Red, but superior to it in quality.

"'Southern Queen' has, with me, proved to be a very good potato, about as early as the Bermudas, productive, of nice shape; is a good keeper, easy to cultivate and dig, although the quality is not of the very best.

"The 'Red Spanish' is of good quality, very productive, and, I think, will supersede some of the less valuable sorts when its qualities are more generally known.

"The 'Yellow' and 'Red Nansemond,' the 'Early York,' and 'Early Jersey,' are all old and standard sorts, and so well known that it is unnecessary for me to describe them. Their quality is first-rate : but they do not. with us, yield equal to some of the newer varieties.

"The 'Mexican,' or 'Bahama Yam,' introduced some few years ago, has the reputation of being a very productive variety. A vigorous grower ; tuber globular ; skin dull white ; pale yellow within ; an early variety, and the best for the table, when first dug, of all this class of tubers. It is said to keep well if properly cared for, and produces large crops."

OTHER VARIETIES.—1st. "Porto Viejo."—Very large, sweet. and abundant : skin, dark-red ; flesh, deep pink.

2nd. "Boca Sagarto."—Not so large, but very sweet, and of better flavor.

3rd. "Nina."—Still better, but rather smaller ; excellent flavor, and very sweet.

These three varieties are very distinct.

1st. Skin, dark-red ; flesh, deep pink.

2d. Skin, light pink : flesh, yellowish white. The average weight of these tubers is about one and one-quarter to one and one-half pound.

3d. Skin and flesh yellowish white.

These potatoes were introduced by M. C. Montjoy, U. S. Consul to Peru, in 1878, being the leading standard varieties of that country.

CHAPTER II.

PRODUCTIVENESS AND PROFITS.

The average productive capacity of the Sweet Potato depends, of course, mainly on soil, climate, and culture. In Brown County, Ohio, Wm. Meyer, Esq., raised on nine rods twenty-three bushels of yellow Sweet Potatoes, at a cost of between five and six dollars. Soil, a light loam, without manure. In Hanover County. Virginia. the average is from one hundred to one hundred and fifty bushels per acre. As high as three hundred bushels have been reached, which, at the average price of seventy-five cents per bushel. would give a return of two hundred and twenty-five dollars per acre. Many planters sell their early select tubers at one dollar per bushel.

The potatoes exhibited at the State Fair at Richmond, in 1877, by Adolphus Talley, Esq., of Hanover County, were of a crop that yielded two hundred and forty-five bushels to the acre.

In Nansemond, Norfolk, and other maritime counties, the average is believed to be still larger. In Georgia three hundred bushels per acre have been raised. Statistics in regard to the Sweet Potato are exceedingly meagre, it not having, heretofore, been a main crop, except in limited districts. This is attributable mostly to ignorance and carelessness in the methods of preservation from decay, rendering profits uncertain, except where navigation and railroad facilities are at hand.

When we shall have devised better means for curing the potatoes for foreign shipment, the increase of production will doubtless be augmented beyond calculation. This being secured, Covent Garden, London, and other great marts of trade, would require vast quantities of this luscious product of the sandy lands of our Southern country ; and, when this is successfully accomplished, the Sweet Potato crop might become as valuable as one-half the cotton crop.

CHAPTER III.

USES OF THE SWEET POTATO.

In the year 1868, C. H. Marshall, of Vicksburg, Miss., forwarded to the Department of Agriculture specimens of Sweet Potatoes dried (varieties not named), and also some converted into meal. In June, 1869, additional samples were forwarded, with the request to have them examined in the laboratory. The specimens, both sliced and flour, were white, the root slices being covered with thin white powder (starch grains) and on cracking the slice across, the center had, in few instances, altered its color. The meal had a slight, yellow-brown tinge. The following is a part of the result of the analysis :

AVERAGE OF TWO ANALYSES.

Moisture 7.95
Organic Matter.................................. 88.90
Ash... 3.15

Organic Matter=89.

Cellulose 6.750
Starch 65.290
Albumen.. 1.214
Sugar 14.830
Fat .... .810
                                              ———
                                              88.894

(We omit the balance of the analysis).

"No fermentation of any kind appears to have been set up in the potato during or since the act of drying ; the vegetable acids are quite readily distinguishable. The grains of starch are irregularly rounded, and smaller even than those of wheat starch. This capability of being dried without alteration, is a feature of great importance, as this material can be a source of food for cattle during the winter months, and, indeed, during times of scarcity, might be used by man. Another point of interest concerning this root, is the large amount of sugar which it yields in the dried state, over fourteen per cent. This sugar is altogether in the form of cane sugar ; if the flour be mixed with cold water, no glucose can be detected in it, and if the dialysing fluid be not heated above one hundred degrees Fahrenheit, no glucose is afforded ; when boiled it begins to appear, and gradually augments. On account of the abundance of the sugar contents, and its condition as cane sugar, this tuber might possibly become a source of sugar manufacture."

Sweet Potatoes, especially those with red skins, yield a considerable quantity of farinaceous matter, which forms a fine, nutritious jelly when mixed with water. "Bowen's Patent Sago" is the powder, which was prepared by a person of the above name, at Savannah, Georgia, chiefly for export to England, for the British army.

The process was similar to that which is well known in Europe, for procuring flour of the common or Irish potato, viz : by grating the clean roots, washing the mass through brass sieves of different sizes, and collecting the starch at the bottom of the vessel which receives the fluid; finally it is dried on pans, either in the sun or by other means.

The late much lamented Dr. G. W. Briggs, of Nansemond Co., Va., who was a popular horticultural writer and farmer, furnished " The American Farmer " the following appreciation of the Sweet Potato :

" One of the most valuable and useful crops grown on the farm for family use; in March, April, and May, when other vegetables are scarce, this is the vegetable indispensable. We make of it potato custards, Sweet Potato pies, spiced with wine sauce, potato pudding, and boiled entire, peeled and sliced, a la Yankee style, (dressed with butter, but no salt, if you please), it is an excellent dish. With us the universal custom is to bake slowly and long, putting them on for dinner soon after breakfast, and sending them to the table hot and in their own skins ; peeled and dressed with butter, or gravy from the roast fowl, few persons will reject them.

" In the exhausting diarrhœa of teething children during the summer, our people use and find roasted Sweet Potatoes an excellent food and a remedy for this disease in their little ones." We think this of great value, and should be widely known, as it suffices both for food and medicine.

" Sliced and dried, they may be sent on long sea voyages, or ground into flour, make excellent bread. We have seen it used to cheapen wheat flour, the boiled potatoes being mixed with it for bread and biscuit.

" The first digging, for family use in summer, should

be exposed to the sun before using to sweeten them. In August and September, in this County, you will find them lying exposed, for this purpose, on the flat shed roof of most farm-houses.

"To cook them, when dried as hard as chips, it is only necessary to pour boiling water over them the night before they are wanted, and next day boil, peel, and dress with butter."

In our estimation nothing can be more palatable than a portion of fat, juicy sirloin of beef, roasted brown, in a large dish surrounded by baked "Yellow Nansemonds," partially immersed in the hot gravy, and smoking on the dining-table!

In this region the yellow varieties are sweetest and best for the table, and are largely cultivated for family use ; and, with the superior modes of keeping practised all through the potato regions, they may be kept in good condition until late in the spring. The new, early sorts, make it easy for those who desire it, to have Sweet Potatoes for table use the year through.

"Sweet Potato Bread."—Take one cupful of mashed Sweet Potatoes ; one cupful of corn-meal ; one cupful of flour ; one cupful of milk ; two eggs ; one teaspoonful of salt ; two teaspoonfuls of baking-powder ; mix quickly, and if too stiff, add more milk ; bake in a hot oven. There is nothing more wholesome or palatable than this bread.

As a luxury and for profit in many sections of the country, the "sweets" have greatly the advantage of the "Irish." Cooked in any way or shape, they are appreciated as one of the blessings and comforts of life that no family can afford to be without, when it is possible to procure them.

CHAPTER IV.

USES OF THE VINES AND LEAVES.

The vines and leaves compose a large and valuable portion of the plant. They should be used for the following reasons :

1st. They are believed to contain all the elements of plant-food and fertility claimed for the Southern Cow Pea, or for Red Clover, and to be superior to these in some respects. When spread upon the soil and turned under, they decompose more readily than either of these, especially when in a green state.

2nd. As food for stock, green or dry, they are considered to be equal to the best hay. and cattle devour them greedily. They are regarded as especially valuable as food for milch cows.

3rd. For mulching fruit trees, when half rotted, they form the very best material, and may be used with equal advantage as mulch for other purposes.

4th. The Sweet Potato vine, for ornamental purposes, is desirable as a plant to grow in the house. It is a rapid grower, and, in house culture, is much more delicate in appearance than when growing out of doors. Select, the earlier the better, a well-ripened tuber of the Red Nansemond variety, known to be a most vigorous grower, eight or ten inches long. and four or five inches in diameter. A dark-colored hyacinth glass is a suitable and pretty holder for the potato. but a common glass fruit can. or small earthen jar. will do. Fill the vessel with rain-water, and stand the potato, stem end uppermost. in the mouth of it, allowing only two or three inches of the potato to go down into the water. Set it in a warm, light place, to sprout. filling up the jar or glass with water as fast as it evaporates. Probably a great many sprouts will start at once, or in quick succession ; break off all but three or four of these, as the vine will, by so doing, be much longer and more luxuriant. Nothing now will be needed for the well-being of the vine, except to keep the vessel filled with rain-water.

CHAPTER V.

ADAPTATION TO LOCALITIES.

The Sweet Potato is not only at home in all the Southern States, but is produced in large quantities in Central New Jersey, Delaware, and Central Illinois. latitude forty degrees : it has also been successfully raised in gardens in nearly the coldest parts of the State of New York, as well as in Maine, Southern Minnesota. at St. Paul, which is in latitude forty-four to forty-five degrees. It is probable that, under northern cultivation, varieties may originate especially adapted to cold climates. so that, were it needful, its profitable cultivation might be extended several degrees of latitude northward. as is said to have happened in Europe with regard to maize, for which it is asserted that forty-six degrees north latitude. was formerly the limit, whereas now it is cultivated nearly to fifty-two degrees.

With a climate and soil such as tide-water Virginia. and other maritime sections. possess. there is no reason why every family should not be abundantly supplied with these nutritious tubers. and should also furnish for market, to a large extent. all less favored sections.

Various portions of the West are well adapted to the

Sweet Potato, and it will grow in almost any part of the
Temperate Zone, in light soil and southern exposure,
with proper care.

In LaFourche Parish, Louisiana, Sweet Potatoes grow
to great perfection. As far north-west as Kent County,
and other parts of Michigan, the soil seems well adapted
to their growth, and the season sufficiently long.

In Florida the Sweet Potato is considered one of the
most valuable of esculent roots. Philosophers say the
Banana is the greatest and cheapest food gift to man, but
the Sweet Potato, as cultivated in Florida, disputes the
palm. It is not only wholesome and nutritious in the
highest degree, but as, to the best varieties, they are delicious as food. Their power of reproduction it is difficult to over-state. We never heard a good farmer at-
tempt to fix a limit to it, and it is well-nigh illimitable.
In the olden time, down in Florida, the prudent planters
grew prodigious quantities, and banking them up in the
fall, allowed the plantation hands to help themselves, *ad
libitum*, for their own use, and occasionally permitted
faithful Sambo to haul them to market on his own account, in the great plantation wagons, from which they
were sold at a mere nominal price per bushel, scarcely
realizing the cost of hauling.

From what we have given above, some idea can be
formed of the adaptability and wide range of this esculent. The general information in regard to the Sweet
Potato, being heretofore limited, and the ignorance in
regard to its propagation, culture, and keeping, have had
a tendency to suppress public inquiry to considerable extent, hence its culture has remained in the back-ground
of horticultural pursuits.

CHAPTER VI.

SUITABLE SOILS AND MANURES.

Although a sandy and loamy soil, and mild climate, are conditions most favorable to the Sweet Potato, yet the wide range in which it is known to flourish, proves that soils of different character will suffice for its profitable production; and, it can not be denied that noble specimens are often grown in various soils, if not cold and heavy; especially if grown on new lands, well prepared, abounding with humus and potash. Even light, slaty soils, with warm exposure and suitable manures, will insure remunerative returns. The Fluvanna County lands, that produce the finest Virginia tobacco, are also well adapted to the Sweet Potato. These lands are light, with a moderate proportion of sand. Other soils of Piedmont, Virginia, especially around Charlottesville, produce fine potatoes, which supply the home market at Charlottesville, and some for export. It is a well established fact as to soil, that a sandy loam is the best, and a stiff clay the worst, for any variety of Sweet Potato.

The fine, and almost impalpable sand, which covers most of the surface that constitutes the market gardening section of Hanover, Va., seldom occurs in other regions, and this peculiarity of soil, that produces the finest of Sweet Potatoes, may not be attainable elsewhere. Still, the best results are often secured in less favored places.

One of our best cultivators says: "For Sweet Potatoes of any variety, select a light piece of land, in only moderately good heart; give a good dressing of wood-ashes only, and there will be but little doubt of a good crop, if kept clean and well ridged up. This ridging up in Sweet Potato culture, is more important than in the cul-

ture of almost any other crop; it is advantageous to
plant on land that was cultivated in other hoed crops
the previous year. A piece of land on which corn
is apt to burn badly, is considered best for Sweet Potatoes ; and it is observed that hot, dry summers, in which
other crops fail, serve to develop this esculent in size,
and in all its sweetness and fine flavor."

A potato grower in Maryland advises those who would
grow good potatoes, at least in his latitude, not to use
animal manures on their crops. He says that the large
market growers of the Peninsula found this out long ago,
but most private growers continue to ruin their Sweet
Potatoes by using stable manure ; and that, in his experience, the best results have been obtained from wood-
ashes, or a compost of wood-ashes and marsh-turf, made
fine, and spread broadcast before plowing. We admit
that the lavish use of crude, coarse, stable manure would
injure the crop, or almost any other crop, but if well-
rotted stable, or barn-yard and stable manure, well pulverized and mixed, were applied judiciously, we appre-
hend good results would always follow. Indeed, this
practice is used extensively, and with obvious advantage,
in places where wood-mould and ashes cannot be obtained.

In Nansemond County, Va., as a fertilizer for the
Sweet Potato, Baltimore stable manure is used to the
value of fifty dollars per acre. This is composted with
an equal bulk of wood-mould in the drill. This manure
costs from one dollar and thirty to one dollar and fifty
cents per cart load of twenty bushels.

Mr. James G. Tinsley, of Hanover, prefers, for the
Sweet Potato, a light, sandy soil, or any soil well mixed
with sand. Stable manure, he says, is the best fertilizer,
and after that, cow-pen manure. In his section, mould
from the woods, and pine-tags, are used in large quantities, the same land being often put in potatoes. He continues, " I never have been able to make good Sweet Po-

tatoes with guano or artificial fertilizers alone ; but it is necessary to supply coarser manure of some kind to mix with it."

" The value of ashes," according to a statement of Dr. Briggs, of Nansemond, "for the potato, or, indeed. for almost any crop, I can testify from experience. Thirty years ago my father grew Sweet Potatoes in twenty or more patches, for Northern markets, and used sloop loads of ashes for several years. His experience was, that the ashes were the cheapest and most enduring fertilizer for the potato crop he ever tried. The leached ashes were used broadcast, about one hundred and twenty bushels to the acre, and cost ten cents per bushel at the Norfolk soap factory. The drills were filled with wood-mould composted with farm-yard manure." A friend of ours, the present season, sold nearly one thousand one hundred barrels from ten acres ; they were heavily manured with stable manure composted with wood-mould.

We extract from a valuable paper on the Sweet Potato, furnished by one of the Farmers' Clubs of Middle Georgia, by Capt. Pope Barrow, of Oglethrope County, the following in regard to fertilizers :

"Sandy loam is the most favorable soil for the growth of this crop, in this section, and it seems to be alike suitable to all varieties. As to manures, the best results in this neighborhood have been obtained by the use of Superphosphate of Lime. In some cases the most astonishing yield has been obtained by the use of one hundred and fifty pounds of Sulphate of Soda, and Nitrate of Soda, i. e., seventy-five pounds of each, per acre. This however, was applied as a top-dressing." Other farmers in Georgia break the ground deep, open wide furrows, put in plenty of well-rotted manure, or some good superphosphate.

The soils used for the Sweet Potato in the alluvial districts of the West and Southwest, we presume, have plenty of humus, potash, and other factors favorable to the production of this esculent in great perfection ; and, we judge, these compensate for sandy loam, and give planters advantages scarcely surpassed in the best potato districts.

———•◦•———

CHAPTER VII.

PROPAGATION OF THE SWEET POTATO.

Propagation, or multiplication, of the Sweet Potato is as varied as with any other plant, and it is effected more readily and to greater extent, than is practicable with many other vegetables. Indeed, there are methods used for this purpose that insure reproduction almost indefinitely.

SEED POTATOES.—As like produces like, the potatoes selected for seed should be short, sound, straight, and smooth, and from three-fourths of an inch, to one and a quarter inch in diameter. When taken from the cellar or pit, they should be carefully handled, and put down immediately, as rough carriage bruises them, and causes rot to commence, which continues afterwards in the bed.

BEDDING THE POTATO.—The Hanover Potato bed generally contains three bushels, or the double beds are made with six, about ten feet long by four broad, facing the south. Larger beds are made for extensive cultivation. The bed is dug about eighteen inches deep, and is filled for six inches with oak leaves, or small corn-stalks, and well watered, and well stamped down with the feet. Manure is then brought fresh from the stable, and applied to the depth of one foot ; and this is covered to the depth of four inches with good mould, generally from the yard (not pine-mould) and powdered, all lumps being removed. In this region the beds are put down from the tenth to the thirtieth of March, and later cold beds without cover are made. The potatoes are generally put down so as not to touch each other, to prevent rot, if it commences in one, from extending to others. The open space above the mould, is covered with hay or pine trash, to exclude the air, and keep all the heat in the bed, and the cover put down close, which is well packed around the edges with the same material. In twenty-four hours the heat may commence rising, and careful attention should now be given, lest the heat be too great. If the weather is good, the bed should be opened about nine A.M., to the warm sun, and closed again at three P.M. If above a milk-warm heat, water should be applied daily for a week or ten days, and if very great, holes should be made with a stake or crowbar, put down every twelve or fourteen inches, and then withdrawn. When the shoots are about three or four inches high, and the weather is warm, the first plants can be drawn carefully, one at a time, with the right hand, the left hand holding the ground firmly, to prevent the potato from being disturbed or drawn up; a sidewise pull is best. In five weeks from putting down beds, the planting should commence, in order to allow room for the second and third growth of sprouts, planting after each shower during the month of May, and to the middle of June, and on northern slopes to the first of July.

The old plan of reproduction is given in " The Complete Gardener and Florist."—" Sweet Potatoes may be raised in the vicinity of New York by means of a hot-bed ; they should be planted whole, early in April, three or four inches deep, and about the same distance apart. [Instead of being placed three or four inches apart, as above directed, they need be only half an inch apart, just so as not to touch each other.] In about a month

2

they will throw up sprouts. When these are three or four inches above ground, if the season is good, part them off from the potato, without disturbing it, which, if suffered to remain, will produce more sprouts for a successive planting ; plant them immediately on ridges or in hills." It was the practice of the late Joseph Cooper, of New Jersey, to set three or four sprouts in a hill or place, for the reason that the rampant growth of vines checked and smothered the growth of weeds, causing less work with the hoe.

A moderate hot-bed, five feet square, put down early in the month of April, with a half-peck of good, sound, Sweet Potatoes placed therein, will produce a succession of rooted sprouts or slips in May and June, which, if planted and managed carefully, will yield about fifteen bushels of Sweet Potatoes.

To Raise Early Potatoes.—A correspondent from the South gives the following mode of obtaining early Sweet Potatoes, which has been practised for twenty years without a failure :

"Early in March I make a hot-bed, by setting up edgewise four planks, or boards, twelve inches wide, and driving down small stakes on the outside to keep them up. I fill this box or frame with fresh horse-manure (if mixed with litter to some extent it will answer), that has been kept dry, tramping it down until it is eight inches deep in the frame. I then cover the manure with rich earth, two inches deep, upon which I spread potatoes or yams thickly, but not touching each other, and cover them with two inches of rich earth. I then raise one side of my frame (the north) six inches, and cover well with four-foot boards, to keep off all rain, until the slips are up. I almost invariably have them up in two weeks, when I take off the cover and water freely with soap-suds or water. Insert the hand, every few days, into the

manure, to see if it is more than agreeably warm to the
hand. If so, uncover for a few days, but do not let it
rain upon the bed before the plants are up, as it would
get too hot. Slips can be obtained in this way so early
that they will have to be protected from the frost, and in
larger quantities from a peck than from a bushel by the
usual method. If well watered, slips may be drawn
every week from the first of April until into July. I set
them out when the ground is dry, and pour half a pint
of water around each slip, and cover with dry earth."

METHOD OF BEDDING SEED POTATOES—(By a Virginia Planter).—"Select some dry time to dig. In the
meantime, procure pine-bark and spread it out in the
sun a day or two, and dry it before you dig. Raise a
mound on the ground wherever you choose to kiln your
potatoes, about a foot high; then put down a layer
of the thickest pine-bark on the mound (perhaps other
bark would answer), and gather your potatoes up the
same evening of the digging, and place them upon the
bark in a sugar-loaf or conical form. When completed,
cover over with dry pine bark compactly; then upon
that put a layer of wheat straw, and cover the whole
with earth. Make a square pen of poles or rails around
the kiln, taking care to raise one side higher than the
other; then put on your roof of boards, so that it will
not leak. Before the winter sets in (but not very soon
after the kiln has been made), uncover and fill tightly
with leaves; then cover again and open in April following, and set out your hot-bed with the most perfect and
sound tubers of medium size. It is not necessary to use
stake-holes, to ventilate, when beds are made in this way;
there will be enough ventilation if you don't put the leaves
on too soon. This is especially the mode for keeping
seed potatoes. The main crop can be preserved in the
same way."

NEW JERSEY SEED BED.—The farther we go North

the greater the necessity for especial care and attention to preserve the Sweet Potato crop from decay, and this is also true as regards seed-beds.

Mr. S. J. Allen, of New Jersey, an extensive cultivator, in sandy soil, gives the following comprehensive directions, as practised by himself, which doubtless would be equally proper for the latitude of New York and further North :

" The potatoes usually selected for seed are of short, compact shape, rather below medium size, and in this latitude are 'sprouted' in hot-beds, and the sprouts, when well-rooted, set in the field. A mild hot-bed should be made for them about the 10th of April. The bed should run east and west. Dig a trench twelve or fifteen inches deep, six feet wide, and of any desired length. A bed one hundred feet long is large enough for about thirty-five bushels of seed, which should yield at first pulling sixty thousand plants, and ten days' later thirty thousand more. Board up the south side of the trench about eighteen inches high ; the other three feet. Manure for the hot-bed should be thrown into a compact heap ten days before needed, being turned over once or twice in the interval, to insure an even commencement of heating, and it should be of such a character as to be sure to heat, but not too violently. A good proportion is, two-thirds good fresh horse, and one-third cow-stable manure. It should be placed evenly in the bed to the depth of twelve or fourteen inches, upon a layer of two inches of coarser manure, and be neatly levelled with a fork, and finished by pressing down with a wide board or door; it must be covered with three inches of sandy soil, upon which the seed potatoes are to be placed evenly, about half an inch apart, and settled to one-half their thickness ; then sprinkle with water, and cover with three inches more of sand. The whole must then be covered with a coating of coarse hay, two feet deep, or

sufficient to protect the bed from any change of temperature, and boards must be provided to keep off rain, sup-
ported by temporary rafters, which are taken off out of
the way in good weather ; on these rafters the boards,
a foot wide, are laid, beginning at the bottom and
overlapping.

"Careful watching is necessary for the first ten days.
Examine thoroughly all parts of the bed every day or
two, by thrusting the finger into the sand, between the
potatoes, below their level. It should feel decidedly
warm, and as long as an even warmth at this point can
be maintained the first ten days, the bed needs no farther
attention.   But it almost always happens that, in three
or four days, some parts will become too hot, and others
too cold.   The warmer places must be thinly covered
during the night ; the cooler should have all the hot mid-
day sun possible, and be covered up warm, and every
effort made to increase the heat.   In cases of extreme
heat, water thoroughly, and with a crow-bar (or sharp
stake), work a double row of three-inch holes, one foot
apart, along the center of the bed, through the manure.
This will have the desired effect in a few hours.

"About ten days after ' putting out,' the bed should
show the white crowns of the plants pushing vigorously
through all parts of the surface, and will thenceforth
need uncovering, during all good days, from nine to four
o'clock, increasing the length of time, and decreasing the
covering as the plants strengthen, until just before setting-
out time, when they should be left uncovered at night
also, to ' harden.'   The bed will need frequent watering,
which is done with the least risk about two P. M.

"All this care is requisite, and, though troublesome
to the inexperienced, it resolves itself into a plain,
straightforward duty with practice, though it may result in partial failure from the slightest cause."

It seems to us that the essential points, or even the full

instructions of Mr. Allen, although on a large scale, could be carried out with but little expense or risk. In Virginia we should expect thousands and thousands of plants with half the trouble.

From the records of a Farmer's Club, in Middle Georgia, we gather the following excellent directions for propagating the Sweet Potato :

"SELECTION OF SEED.—First. Always select the largest and best potatoes for seed. It is a great mistake to select small potatoes to bed, expecting to raise large ones. In corn, in cotton, in small grain, all farmers save the best for seed, and potatoes form no exception. With them, as with all other crops, the best results are obtained from the best seed, other things being equal.

"Second. For your bed, select a good, warm, rich spot. Take a spade and cut out a place, or trench, say from fifteen to eighteen inches deep, and three feet wide. Fill this with good stable manure, which should be saturated with water (but not too much), after putting it in the trench. Cover this with about two inches of pulverized soil, and upon this spread the potatoes, just thick enough to prevent them from touching each other ; cover them from one-half to one inch thick with broom straw, to prevent the potatoes from drawing out with the slips, and, upon the straw, place a layer of soil from two and a half to three inches deep. If the weather is cold, make the soil deeper, and scrape it off when it moderates.

"Third. To prepare the land for planting, run off your rows from three and a half to four feet apart, with a medium-sized shovel-plow, and in the bottom of this furrow deposit what manure you intend to use. On the shovel-furrow throw a list with a common one-horse turning-plow, running on both sides of the furrow. Leave the land in this condition until you have your slips drawn and ready to set out, then complete the bed by throwing up two more turning-plow furrows; open this with a narrow ripper, and set your slips from eighteen to twenty inches apart."

CHAPTER VIII.

PREPARATION OF THE SOIL.

Success with the Sweet Potato, as with all other root crops, depends not only on proper soil, but mainly on its preparation and the after culture. Light, sandy, or slaty soils, if these are well drained, naturally or artificially, need not be very deeply stirred; but other or heavy soils should be broken deeply. This, in such soils, not only aids in drainage, but also in warmth, the two most important requisites with the Sweet Potato. These soils should be fallowed in the fall, and they should be replowed in the spring. All soils should be well harrowed and pulverized just previous to ridging or laying off for planting.

Mr. William F. Massey, a most valuable correspondent of the "American Farmer" (Baltimore), says: "In preparing for the Sweet Potato crop, select a piece of light soil that has been in a hoed crop the previous season; plow it not deeper than three inches; harrow and roll, and, with the plow, throw the soil into shallow ridges three feet apart. Flatten the tops of the ridges with a light hand-roller, and set the plants a foot apart (most planters set from fourteen to eighteen inches apart). The subsequent cultivation consists of one 'bar-plowing' and twice ridging with the plow."

For a more Northern latitude, including New Jersey, the following are the preparatory steps for planting: In these latitudes the plants should be ready to set at any time from the middle of May to the first of June, the earlier the better, if the soil is in proper condition as to warmth and moisture. The plants are generally set eighteen inches apart, or less ; this is most conveniently done with a small, light hoe in the shape of a grubbing-hoe ; blade six inches in length by about three in width, and handle one foot long. This hoe is in shape similar to a carpenter's foot-adze, and with it the holes or places for the plants are made with great facility. They also have a new planting machine, now coming into use, which we are not prepared to describe.

In planting, the dry tops of the ridges are removed with a light scraper, drawn by a horse or man, wide enough to do two rows at once, but only as fast as needed by the workmen. Some attach a rolling marker, which facilitates the work very much. With this the ridges should be cut off or levelled to the width of eight or ten inches. This also destroys the first incipient crop of weeds, which is very important, and leaves the moist earth in good condition for setting the plants. In this way the work is well done and with great rapidity.

Instead of ridges, it is the practice of some farmers further South, if the soil is sandy or light, after the land is well prepared, to lay off the rows about three or three and a half feet apart each way, with a single-horse turn-plow ; then throw up a furrow each side of these rows each way, as in hilling for tobacco ; it is then light work to form good-sized hills with the weeding-hoe. If the soil is not rich or suitable, they run a furrow each way, as above, and at the intersection of the rows a good shovelful of suitable manure is put in the places. The manure used may be fine wood-earth, mixed with ashes ; or, if this cannot be had, any rich soil, well-mixed with fine stable manure, will answer. The manure being in place, the loose soil around is pulled up with weeding-hoes, so as to form a good medium-sized hill on the manure. When ready to plant, the tops of these hills are cut off with a weeding-hoe, and the plants set in the center of the flattened tops. This mode requires less labor, and some farmers think produces larger crops. When the planting is done in this way, the after cultivation is, much less difficult, as the young weeds can be kept down with comparative ease with the plow and hoe, and with much less hand-weeding, and there is a great saving of manure.

CHAPTER IX.

DRAWING THE PLANTS AND PLANTING.

How to Draw the Sets.—When the plants are about three or four inches high, and the weather warm, the first sets can be drawn carefully, one at a time, with the right hand, the left holding the ground firmly to prevent the potato from being drawn out. In five weeks from the time of putting down the beds, the planting should commence, in order to allow room for the second and third growth of sprouts, planting after each shower during the month of May to the middle of June and on the northern slope of land, to the first of July. This applies to Hanover County, Va., and to the upper counties.

Preparing the Sets.—Although plants do well without any preparation, yet it adds much to their vigor and healthy growth to treat them as follows : Dip them in a thick paste of fresh cow-stable manure and fine mould mixed with water; then dibble the plants fifteen inches apart in the ridge, and as deep as possible, so as not to cover the bud. "Draws" or "sets," when six inches high, are of about the right size to plant.

Some planters say the hand is much better than anything else to set with, and by this means the setting is more expeditiously done by boys of from twelve to sixteen years than by grown persons, as they are more supple and have less bending of the back. Some use the short-handled hoe already described; others use the transplanting-trowel for making the holes or places for the sets. In planting when the weather is dry, as we sometimes are compelled to do, the hills for the plants should be watered with about a pint or a little less for each hole. When the water has subsided, the plants are set, and the soil firmly pressed around each one. The next evening the same quantity of water should be poured in a circle around the plant. Thus treated, it is rarely that any will be lost. It is a good rule never to list or prepare more rows or hills than can be set in one day, as the plants live better in fresh soil.

PLANTING SETS.—"Just as early as the plants can be safely risked in the open field, say the last of April (in the climate of Nansemond, Va., to the middle of May), draw the plants from the bed, and set them on the fresh, newly-prepared ridges or hills. If, when ready to plant, showery weather comes on, we avail ourselves of it, and at once set the plants. If we are ready, and do not desire to defer the setting, we draw the plants, set the roots, as drawn, in boxes containing mud of the consistence of cream; take them to the field and plant late in the evening, firming the earth with the hand by pressing it around each plant as it is set. Well-grown plants possess so many fibrous roots and live so easily in freshly-moved soil, that they often seem to do better in this way than when set after very hard rains, when the soil was too wet ; in such condition it will bake hard around the plants. In general, women or boys drop the sets at the proper distance (say fifteen or eighteen inches apart), each followed by the hand who plants.

CHAPTER X.

IMPLEMENTS USED IN SWEET POTATO CULTURE.

The tools required in the production of the Sweet Potato crop are very few and inexpensive. The usual farm tools, such as plows, harrows, spades, shovels, weeding-hoes, rakes, etc., are used for this purpose. Thomas' Smoothing Harrow is recommended in the early stages of cultivation. For setting the plants the Jersey growers are very expert. With a pair of wooden tongs, made of laths, they pick up the plant, insert it, and with a gentle tap the plant is set without the fatigue of stooping.

Mr. Allen, of New Jersey, uses a light Scraper and Marker, drawn by one horse, which not only levels and brushes off the top of the ridges, but effectually destroys the first crop of weeds, and leaves the tops of the ridges just right for planting—and the work is done with great rapidity.

Another device for this purpose, described on another page, is still more simple and inexpensive. It consists of a piece of scantling, two by three inches, and six feet long, drawn by a horse walking between two rows. The marking off is expeditiously done by a boy with a forked stick, with the points fifteen to eighteen inches apart, or the desired distance apart on the ridges may be guessed at by a good dropper.

The short-handled hoe, for opening holes for the sets, is a great convenience. It is in the shape of a grubbing hoe or carpenter's adze. The blade is six inches long (very light) by three inches wide, and the handle twelve inches long. If the soil is sandy or light, the hand will answer this purpose as well. To turn the vines a stick about five feet long, with a hook, is used, to save the labor of stooping. With this the vines are easily pulled to one side or from one valley to the other, without bruising.

In harvesting, the vines are turned aside with the plow, then cut from the ridges or hills with a sharp weeding-hoe. Baskets or hampers of white-oak splits or willow are provided for use in harvesting.

———◦◦———

CHAPTER XI.

CULTIVATION.

The much-lamented Dr. G. W. Briggs, of Nansemond Co., Va., late associate editor of the "Petersburg Rural Messenger," gave some valuable directions in regard to the Sweet Potato. In one of his articles on cultivation, we find the following excellent remarks :

He says, incidentally : "The methods and preparations for planting are various. In this section, ridges or hills over the manure are preferred (except when the manure is broadcast)," as he described in a former article. "In many parts of our own and other States, where farmers plant only for family use, I have often seen high ridges thrown up with the plow, and then the earth carefully pulled up with the weeding-hoe, and the sets planted on the ridge. This we regard as labor lost, and positively injurious to the development of short, thick, marketable roots. The ridge is but a convenience for working the crop,* and when we lay it by, there are very slight elevations, in fact, only fresh earth enough to well sustain the crown of the plants,

"In cultivation, we deem it important to get a good stand as early as possible ; hence, in a few days after planting, we go over the field and replant all that have failed ; next we hand or hoe-work around the sets, loosening the earth, to set them growing.

" We will suppose that the plants are well-rooted, growing, and the grass is springing up around and between the sets ; the sooner we work now, the less will be the labor required.

" With a one-horse plow, the plants are sided off close, and the grass removed with the hand and weeding-hoe ; others prefer flat-weeding the ridges without plowing, scraping down the ridges with the hoe. Sometimes I have saved labor by using the Dixon cotton-sweep, held slanting, so as to shave off the grass into the balk, leaving a very narrow strip on the ridge for the hoe. The crop should be cleaned and worked, and the best method of doing it will suggest itself to the farmer on inspecting the land. In two weeks, more or less, the crop will again require working with hoes and plows, and the balks should be thoroughly worked, so as to destroy the grass.

" At the last working, the vines have grown so much that we turn them into the opposite rows, work thoroughly every other row with the cotton-plow, and then turn

---

* NOTE.—In regard to " high or low ridges," there is difference of opinion. We think, in soils that are rather moist, and consequently cold, and in soils further North, considerable ridges are best ; as, by this means, both warmth and dryness are, in a great degree, secured, which, in our opinion, are important factors, if not essential to successful culture. In the hot sandy soils of Nausemond low ridges might do best.

back, working the rows in which the vines were first placed. To turn the vines, our men use a stick about five feet long, with a hook, to save the labor of stooping; with this they pull the vines easily, without bruising them, from one valley, or balk, to the other." (A light, four-tined, pronged hoe, used as a rake for destroying incipient weeds, is also used for this purpose).

"In a very short time, the vines run from one ridge or hill to the other, and cover the whole surface, and the land will, or ought to, be nearly level as soon as the loose earth settles. The potato roots ought to be so near the top soil that, in August, when we walk over the patch or field, the ground can be seen cracking, where the roots are forming around the stem of the mother plant.

"My impression is that too deep covering of soil will injure the development and size of the roots; and failure is often attributed to soil when, in truth, it is due to improper management and cultivation.

"It frequently happens, in cloudy and rainy seasons, that the vines root of their own accord in the balks, forming little clips, so that many persons go over the ground and break their connection with the soil."

NEW JERSEY CULTURE.—The cultivation should commence just before the weeds make their appearance. For this purpose some recommend a one-horse Thomas' Smoothing Harrow, "a round" to a row; sometimes it is best to remove one tooth, to allow the remainder to straddle the row at that point. This is Mr. Allen's mode. He recommends for the next working the use of a broad-toothed cultivator, and the next also, and a careful hoeing between these two operations. Soon after the last working, if the growth of the vines is rampant, it will be necessary to turn the vines out of the way, as practised by Dr. Briggs, working every other balk, and turning back and finishing. (" Balks, or middles, are the spaces left unplowed after throwing one furrow to each row.")

When the vines begin to meet and occupy the middles, they are about ready for the last working. For this purpose, they are to be pulled out of the way to one side, throwing the vines of two rows together. The rows are then plowed out, or from, and scraped, to destroy the weeds, with the weeding-hoe. Then plowed to, and the middle parts plowed out. All this should be done in proper time ; if delayed, it will soon require much irksome labor to put the crop in good condition for growth.

GEORGIA CULTURE.—The ground being well prepared, run off your rows three and a half or four feet apart, with a shovel-plow, and, in the bottom of this furrow, deposit whatever manure you intend to use, unless the soil is sufficiently rich. Then, on the shovel-furrow, throw a list with a common one-horse turn-plow, running on both sides of the furrow. Leave the land in this condition until you are ready to plant ; then complete the bed or ridge, by throwing up two more turning-plow furrows ; open this with a light, narrow ripper, and set slips eighteen to twenty inches apart.

Four or five days after transplanting, work the plants with a weeding-hoe, giving them a little loose soil, at the same time open the middles with one furrow of a shovel-plow. This is the first working. The second, side the beds with a shovel, and open the middles with a turn-plow, brushing around the vines with a weeding-hoe, to keep the earth off of them. The third and last working is performed by plowing out the middles with a sweep, and hoeing the bed or ridge, pulling the earth to the vines, but not covering them, as this will cause them to take root and make a late crop of fibrous roots that are worthless, besides the loss of nutriment they draw from the larger tubers. Of course, no potato gathered before it is ripe can be kept sound. They should be dug after the frost has partially killed the vines.

ANOTHER MODE.—Another Georgia farmer gives his mode of cultivation and preparation of the ground, in the subjoined report of a crop which he entered for a premium at the Georgia State Fair :

" Broke the land in March, with a one-horse turn-plow, six inches deep. Ran off the rows three feet apart, on the 1st of May, with a turning-shovel. Bedded with the same plow the other way, making the rows three feet apart. Made small hills with a hoe, by drawing up the soil lightly from the corners of the beds or squares between the furrows. Opened the tops of the hills with the hoe ; put crushed cotton seed in each hill, at the rate of fifteen bushels to the acre, and covered the seed with earth. (Think the cotton seed did but little good, if any.) Bedded out my Sweet Potatoes first day of April. Transplanted my slips from the middle of May to the first of June. Plowed twice with sweep, two furrows to each row, and hoed once. Went over the patch (one acre) in August with a narrow hoe, and broke the vines loose from the ground, where they had taken root between the hills. Dug the patch October 15th. Yield two hundred and fifty-four bushels and thirty pounds.*

Mr. C. M. Cullen, of Hanover, Va., (in " Richmond Planter and Farmer "), says in regard to cultivation : "The ridges are thrown up from three to three and a half feet apart, and just before planting the ridge is raked down with a hoe or rake, or, better still, by the scantling implement, a piece of scantling two by three inches, and six feet long, drawn by a horse walking be-

*NOTE.—E. P. Meredith, Esq., of Hanover County, Va., says : "The full productive capacity of our lands have never been reached, producing, in some cases, as much as three hundred bushels per acre of potatoes."

tween two rows. The marking off may be done by a boy with a forked stick, the points twenty inches apart; or the distance may be guessed by a good dropper, as heretofore directed.

" The cultivation should be done with a good cultivator—hoe work; and at the last working the vines are thrown over on each side alternately. If there is no disease or insects, the plants grow off at once. If the cut-worm, or any other insect is present, replanting is necessary. If the "black-root" is perceptible, the sprouts should not be planted. Sometimes there is no appearance of this disease in the beds, but it becomes apparent in the field; some persons ascribe the disease to overheat in the bed, others to damp, cold weather, but there is nothing definite known about the cause.

" The potato generally grows about one inch in diameter a month, and sometimes the larger ones are dug by the first of September, to obtain higher prices. The yams grow faster, but do not sell as well by thirty per cent. In this region, from the 16th to the 26th of October, the bulk of the potato crop is dug, and averages, according to fertility of soil and the proper cultivation, from seventy-five to one hundred and fifty bushels to the acre."

EXTERMINATION OF WEEDS.—Weeds are a great pest in all branches of horticulture. The best way to manage them is to give the crops timely and frequent cultivation. A single stroke with a steel garden-rake will kill thousands as they begin to show themselves above ground in the truck patch; or, in field culture, a single passage of a light, close-set harrow, sweeping beside the plants, will effectually kill or suppress their rampant growth, and put a stop to their exhaustive demands on the soil intended for other uses. But let them get a start, and to head them or behead them will require more scraping, pulling, and hoeing than any gardener can afford to give in a busy season.

It is often hard to beat this truth into the heads of laborers. Incipient weeds can be kept under with one-fourth the labor that will be required if allowed to attain the hight of a few inches. Large beds can be raked out in a few minutes, which, if neglected, would require hours, to say nothing of the damage and set-back sustained by the cultivated crop.

Sweet Potato crops are especially liable to damage from weeds. When neglected, weeds soon get the advantage, and double the labor is required to suppress the.n. They spring up close around the plant, and hand-weeding is the only remedy.

CHAPTER XII.

HARVESTING THE SWEET POTATO.

How to Dig.—With the two-horse plow ; pass between the rows to collect the vines ; with a sharp weeding-hoe (ground for this purpose), cut the vines from the ridges or hills, and have them carried out of the way ; then side down and put in the plow deep, and turn them all out. The potatoes will come up in bunches or clusters, and with the bottom ends projecting out of the furrow-slice. They are, with the plow, saved in half the time, and with scarcely any of them cut or broken. With a pronged hoe or potato-hook they are quickly taken out of the loose ground and placed in the heaping row. The soil is then rubbed or shaken from the potatoes, and they are deposited in white oak-split or willow baskets or hampers, and removed from the field. The sorting is generally done in the field, making three lots —market roots, cut and broken roots, and small roots or slips.

CONDITION FOR HOUSING.—Few crops are more susceptible to injury by cold and frost than the Sweet Potato. Careless farmers often allow the crop to remain in the ground in the fall, until the frost has killed the vines. When such is the case, many potatoes will be found with frosted ends; such will be bitter when cooked, and will decay easily. Some of our experienced growers say that to keep well, the roots should be harvested while growing, before the frost touches the vines. If nearly matured, doubtless this would be right. Warmth—say seventy degrees—darkness and dryness, are conditions we must look for, with an equitable temperature. Pleasant dry days in October are preferred for putting the potatoes into the house or kiln.

The proper condition of the potatoes, as to dryness or moisture, is very important, and an unsettled point. It is the custom, when they are for early market or for early family use, to dry them in the sun on sheds or other convenient places. For market, before storing, it is the practice of some experienced growers to dry them in the shade a few days before they are put away. Others equally capable of judging say: "Directly the digging and sorting is over, which should be in dry weather, take them up in hampers and house them in bulk, whilst they are plump and fresh." If they are put away in sand or dry earth in this condition, and properly protected from cold, doubtless it is the best mode for their preservation. Potatoes put away in this order have been known to keep until the middle of May —and, when the sand was taken out in October to refill with another crop, potatoes were found that had been there a year, and as sound as those dug on that day. Their preservation or decay, doubtless, depends mainly on the temperature and the exclusion of the atmosphere and light.

YIELD AND PROFIT.—A correspondent of the "Amer-

ican Farmer " writes : " So many factors enter here in
reference to the land and its adaptation to the crop, and
the time of the harvest and supply in the market, that
it is almost impossible even to approximate results. The
potato is edible as soon as it has any considerable size,
and will continue to grow until frost, often a month or
six weeks longer than it is permitted to do when sold in
August as an early market crop.

" A grower remarked to me, some time since, that
when he could harvest twenty-five barrels per acre in August, and get three dollars per barrel, he was satisfied it
paid him well.

" Such a crop would yield more than forty barrels per
acre in October. The profit will depend, like other
crops, on the yield per acre and market price ; in general, it is always well worth the labor, and a good rent of
land for home consumption and home markets : by the
latter, I refer to Virginia towns—Lynchburg, Danville,
Charlottesville, Staunton, and other interior towns
through which there is railroad transportation from the
lower counties "

CHAPTER XIII.

TRANSPORTATION AND MARKETING.

The facilities for the transportation and disposal of
the Sweet Potato crop are not less ample than those for
other crops. The seaboard counties, all along the Southern coast, in many places have rivers, creeks, small bays,
and inlets, that admit sloops and small trading vessels
almost to the very doors of the truckers and farmers.
This is especially the case as regards the Chesapeake Bay
and other expanded waters, and also the numerous riv-

ers, both large and small, suitable for coasting vessels. These tidewater farmers, or truckers, plant and raise largely, not only Sweet Potatoes, but other vegetables and also fruits, in great abundance, for which their climate and soil are so well adapted; these are shipped to northern markets, with moderate or reduced freight expenses and commissions, or they are sold upon the spot. The county of Nansemond, Va., has a light and friable soil, abounding in the richest and most accessible deposits of shell and marl, with water navigation which gives every man a wharf and a market on his own farm; yet these lands, with all these advantages, and after they have been well-limed, can frequently be bought at low prices, and, in many instances, with good buildings. Nothing can be finer than the water prospect from some of the old settlements on the Nansemond river. A broad sheet of water at one's feet, gradually expands into the magnificent Hampton Roads of historic fame, whilst, as far as the eye can reach, the trading craft may be seen looking for truck in the Nansemond and neighboring creeks. So accessible are these situations, that the northern hucksters float their warehouses, in the shape of sloops and schooners, to the point of production, and hang out their signs from the mast-head: "Potatoes Wanted;" "Peaches Wanted;" "The Highest Prices Given for Watermelons, Fruits, Vegetables, etc." Such are the cries of Nansemond.

But the tidewater sections of Virginia are not the only accessible points that abound with the delightful prospect of oysters, crabs, and Sweet Potatoes. Like advantages are to be found on the coast as far as New Jersey, and South to the capes of Florida. All up the Lower Mississippi and the Ohio Valleys, the potato is grown to perfection, and shipped to market by means of river and railroad transportation, with the other products of the country.

PACKING.—Sweet Potatoes are generally shipped in three-bushel barrels, usually flour barrels. The potatoes are rubbed, but not bruised, to remove the sand or dirt. They are then packed in the barrels, and the open end secured by tacking over it a coarse cloth, instead of putting in the head, just as grapes are sent in casks to the wine cellars.

PRODUCT PER ACRE.—The usual product per acre is put at from twenty-five to forty-five barrels, according to culture, soil and climate. Forty barrels is not unusual. "A friend of ours, last season, sold nearly one thousand one hundred barrels from ten acres. The ground was heavily manured with stable manure, composted with wood-mould and ashes."

CHAPTER XIV.

STORING AND KEEPING.

HOW TO KEEP SWEET POTATOES.—James R. Wilson, of Bolivar County, Miss., writes: "At the South, where a dry, well-constructed cellar is rarely seen, Sweet Potatoes are frequently stored for keeping in the following manner: A flue, say eight feet high, is built of lattice, upon ground slightly elevated, where water cannot settle, and around this flue forty or fifty bushels of potatoes are piled in a conical heap or shape. Over these a covering of three or four inches of straw is spread, and over the straw, earth. This last covering is graduated to suit the weather; at first it is light, and then deeper, as the temperature falls. Rough sheds are erected over each heap, and in cold weather the top of the flue is

covered with straw. The potatoes are dried, after digging
and before storing, by exposure to the air (not to the
sun) a few hours. No potatoes that are bruised or cut
are put in the heap. It is quite probable this mode
would not prove successful at the North, but I give it for
what it is worth to southern readers."

Doubtless Mr. Wilson's mode would prove successful
in the South, or in all potato regions south of him. The
plan is very simple and cheap.

A first-class Sweet Potato house in New Jersey is now
built of stone, one-half under and one-half above
ground, though banked to the eaves, with an entry
through the center, in which the stove is placed. The
bins are from six to eight feet square, and eight to twelve
deep. The house is sixteen by eighteen feet inside, with
walls ten feet high, five feet of which are above the level
of the ground, but banked to the eaves. There is a glass
door on the south, with a window above. This house
holds three thousand bushels : when full, three thousand
five hundred bushels. It is plastered from the wall up to
the peak, with lathing on the under side of the rafters.

The main crop is usually dug after a very slight frost
has touched the vines—cutting them off the vines, plowing out, and "shaking off" three rows together. For
market, the potatoes are then "rubbed off," and put up
in baskets, in two sizes. For winter sales they are picked
without rubbing off, and poured into large bins in a
house or cellar, with a constant fire, especially during
the sweating period. The best temperature is about
sixty degrees.

OTHER WAYS OF KEEPING.—"I have noticed for the
last few years various plans for preventing Sweet Potatoes
from rotting after being gathered and banked and
housed. It was my father's plan to wait until the frost
had partially killed the vines, and dig on a good, open

day, throwing in heaps, after dividing the large from the small—turning all about—then to haul up to a place rather sloping, and the earth dug out to a hard foundation ; the potatoes were put on the ground and covered with corn-stalks long enough to go from the bottom of the trench to the top of the bank, with small ones to fill up the cracks, so that you could not see the potatoes at all ; they then commenced at the bottom to cover with earth, so there would be a good thickness of it all the way up (using no straw or bark), leaving the top open, and put a good shelter over it, to cover the entire bank. I never knew of any potatoes to be lost under any circumstances, managed as above. Now, let all make a trial of this plan, and see for themselves if it is not a good one."—McDuffie, in "Southern Cultivator."

A correspondent of the "North Carolina Farmer" gives his mode : "The first thing to be done in order to raise good potatoes, as in all other crops, is to drain the land thoroughly. The better the land is drained the better the potatoes will be to eat, the better they will yield, and the better they will keep. The great secret, or luck, as it is often termed, in keeping potatoes, is in having the land on which they are raised dry—made so by draining whenever it is necessary. If they are raised on such land, there is no difficulty in keeping them. There are three things to be observed, viz. : Neither to let them get too hot, or too cold, or too wet. To keep them from getting too cold, if put up in hills for keeping, protect them by putting plenty of earth around them, except at the top of the hill (where a vent is left until danger of getting too cold, when it should be closed), but con-, siderable cold may occur before this would become necessary ; then cover well with straw or leaves, or, in other words, keep all parts of the hill or mound, from top to bottom, well covered to keep out the cold, with the hole uncovered in mild weather to let out the heat. Many a hill of potatoes heats from having too much strain on the top, and many a hill freezes from not having earth enough around the bottom. The opening of the top of the hill should always be left uncovered until the potatoes are thoroughly cured, whether kept in houses or out of doors."

WINTERING IN SUSSEX COUNTY, VA.—They dig pits underneath their top-fodder stacks, which are in the shape of an A, or a housetop with a square roof. These pits are from one and a half to two feet deep, and as wide as the stack will admit—the length from fork to fork that supports the top pole of the stack. Before storing the potatoes away, they have the sides and ends of the pits well planked up, and the bottoms covered about two inches thick with pine beard (pine tags). They also have a layer of pine beard up the sides and ends, about the same thickness as that which covers the bottom. This layer is placed along as the potatoes are packed away, the pits being nearly filled with potatoes. They are then covered over lightly with pine beard, and the covering finished with poles and earth which is to be thrown on last, lightly, taking care to stop the apertures between the poles, so that no earth can pass through. In this way hundreds of bushels in pits are kept without the loss of five. Care should be taken before storing away potatoes for winter markets or home use, to have them carefully picked over, and all such as are cut, broken, or bruised, thrown out ; to avoid bruising potatoes much, they should be handled carefully and lightly. With a view to keep potatoes in this way, stacks may be made up on elevated places, so that the water may pass off without soaking into the ground—thereby the pits are kept perfectly dry, which is all-important.

Out of a large quantity of potatoes kept in this way, there was not a half bushel injured.

3

We know that these tubers can be kept in excellent condition until late in the spring, by the means above recommended, but fodder-stacks are now seldom made so as to admit a potato pit, as it is the custom to cut up corn with stalk and fodder, and have a solid stack. But shelters and pits could be cheaply made in the same shape as an old-fashioned fodder-stack, that would answer the same purpose.

CHAPTER XV.

DISEASES AND ENEMIES OF THE SWEET POTATO.

The most formidable enemy to the young plants in the hot-bed, appearing later in the field soon after transplanting, is the "black root," "black rot," or "black shank," familiar to growers. It is a kind of blight or gangrene of the roots, and the general impression is that it proceeds from over-stimulation by heat and ammonia, from the material used in the bed ; it sometimes, although rarely, appears in the plants raised under sash in cold frames. Soon after setting the plants, we find they do not grow, leaves look yellow, spotted and sickly ; pulling up the set, we find the cause in the black stems under the earth, in which there is very little life and circulation. The remedy is of course prevention, and a careful rejection of all plants affected with black spots on the stems when drawn from the propagating beds. When the plants are healthy, setting over heating manure, may cause it, or cold, unfavorable weather supervening soon after they are set, so that plants cannot grow, is supposed to be another cause of this disease.

Others describe the "black rot" as the rotting off of the sprouts from the potato in the beds, or showing an occasional sprout with black spots on the otherwise white stem and roots. It is regarded as a capricious disease, depending upon the weather and other causes.

Ants often undermine plants in the ridges or hills, and do some mischief, as do cut-worms. The remedy is frequent hoeing. The striped-bug is sometimes troublesome. This is easily managed by sowing air-slacked lime on the vines. There are also small, whitish-yellow, mealy insects called "peddlers," that feed on the leaves, they work entirely upon the under side of the leaves, and seldom do much harm. Dusting with Paris green when the leaves are wet or damp, it is supposed, would put them to rout.

Just here the Sweet Potato has the advantage of most other plants, and, especially of the common or Irish potato. In fact, it has two advantages over that tuber. It is seldom molested by bugs or worms, and it will grow and thrive in warm, dry soils, where the common potato would wither and perish for want of coolness and moisture.

No insect, so far, has troubled the Sweet Potato to damage it to any extent. If the bugs continue to destroy the common potato, as in years past, we will have to turn our attention more to the growing of the Sweet Potato to fill its place. [While Virginia is fortunate in being free from the insects that injure the Sweet Potato vine, farther West, especially in Missouri, they are attacked by several species of Tortoise Beetles, mostly of the genus *Cassida*. The larva is armed with numerous spines, and has the unpleasant habit of covering its back with a shield of its own excrement. The perfect insects, which also feed on the vines, have the wing covers and thorax so extended as to give them a strong resemblance to a miniature tortoise; some of them are exceedingly beautiful, with golden and other metallic tints. They will be found figured in Prof. C. V. Riley's Second Report on the Insects Injurious to Missouri (1869). As the insects are mainly upon the under-sides of the leaves, the application of poison to destroy them is difficult. Examining the plants while young and picking off all the insects that may be found, is recommended as the better remedy.—Ed.]

———

CHAPTER XVI.

USEFUL TABLES, ETC.

WEIGHT OF AGRICULTURAL PRODUCTS.—Weight of a bushel as established by the laws of the United States :

	lbs.		lbs.
Sweet Potatoes	55	Castor Beans	46
Irish Potatoes	60	Dried Peaches	33
White Beans	60	Dried Apples	26
Peas	60	Onions	57
Turnips	55	Onion Sets	35
Ground Beans	24		

CAPACITY OF BOXES.

A box 20 inches square and $16\frac{1}{2}$ inches deep will contain 1 barrel (3 bushels).

A box 15 inches square and $14\frac{1}{2}$ inches deep will contain 1 half barrel.

A box 17 inches by 14 inches and 9 inches deep will contain 1 bushel.

A box 10 inches by 12 and 9 inches deep will contain one-half bushel.

A box 8 inches square and $8\frac{2}{3}$ inches deep will contain 1 peck.

NUMBER OF PLANTS FOR ONE ACRE.

Sweet Potatoes	1½ foot by	3	feet	9,600
" "	1½ foot by	3½ feet		8,100
Strawberries	1 foot by	3	feet	14,530
Raspberries	6 feet by	6	feet	1,210
Dwarf Pears	12 feet by	12	feet	302
Quinces	15 feet by	15	feet	193

NUMBER OF SQUARE FEET IN AN ACRE, 43,590; 70 yards wide by 69 long, one acre.

STANDARD FRUIT MEASURES.—We have long needed standard measures for selling fruits and vegetables. A "basket" has never meant anything positive, and the artful way in which baskets have been filled by raising the bottoms, etc., has been a source of much fraud to buyers. The Fruit Packers' Board of Trade, at Baltimore, Md., the members of which purchase large quantities of peaches and tomatoes, recently adopted a standard measure, as follows:

" That the standard bushel for peaches shall be a box 9 inches deep, 14 inches wide, and 22½ inches long, in the clear, with half-inch partition; that the standard half bushel for tomatoes shall be a basket 10 inches deep, 10½ inches across the bottom, and 15 inches across the top; and that the barrel for measuring peas shall hold not less than 2½ standard bushels.

' An ordinary bushel box for apples, etc., is 15½ inches long, inside, 14 inches wide, and 12 inches deep in the clear. The ends may be of ¾-inch boards; bottom slats same; side and top slats 1½ inch wide by ½ inch thick, allowing spaces between of one inch, more or less, according to the description of the fruit to be shipped. The boards should be of light material—white pine or poplar."

POTATO BARRELS.—The Norfolk dealers in Sweet Potatoes ship in flour barrels, with a coarse, strong cloth tacked over in place of the head. This gives ventilation and is sufficiently secure.

TAPE LINES.—Every gardener or farmer should provide himself with a tape-line, so that he may know the size of his patches, lots, and fields, how much seed they need, what they yield, etc. A measure always at hand and properly used, will be to him as important as is a compass to the mariner.

MEASURING POLES.—The farmer should always keep a pocket rule, a yard-stick, and poles of 6 feet, 10 feet, and one of 16'/$_2$ feet, or one rod ; the last to be made of any light wood, graduated or tapered each way from the center to the ends, with marks for each foot of length.

CHAPTER XVII.

CONCLUSION.

In conclusion we would remind farmers and planters that the Sweet Potato can endure more heat and drouth than any other root crop. Turnips, parsnips, carrots, beets, etc., succumb and wither at a time when the conditions are just right for this crop. Hence our dry and hot seasons, which seem to increase in their torrid character, produce this splendid esculent in the highest perfection, and we may rely upon this when all other root crops fail. This should induce all who have the proper soil to plant the Sweet Potato freely for home use, if not for market.

The apparent obstacle to its culture is the difficulty in the preservation of the crop for winter use. This is mostly due to a want of knowledge, as the means are always at hand, in any climate, for keeping them in excellent condition until late the following spring.

The Sweet Potato will grow, thrive, and mature, despite of the driest and hottest weather, and there is scarcely any other esculent that will do this under a burning sun and torrid atmosphere. In this work we have given the various modes of culture, and the most approved methods for the preservation of the tubers, as practised in widely different sections from New York to Texas. To preserve the crop, different localities require more or less protection, according to climate. If due attention is paid to this there need be no failure, and but little loss if each section adopts modes of culture and keeping suitable to its latitude.

There can be no doubt that a vast increase of wholesome and nutritious food would be secured should the people within the wide range in which it may be cultivated be made to see the great value of the Sweet Potato as an adjunct to the ordinary roots and cereals in increasing the resources of human food.

CHAPTER XVIII.

THE CHINESE YAM.

(*Dioscorea Batatas.*)

This esculent, having in its manner of growth and uses, much in common with the Sweet Potato, may be with propriety noticed in this work. It belongs to the same genus, *Dioscorea*, with the tropical yams, which are much used as food in warm countries, their large farinaceous roots serving as a substitute for potatoes. These, *Dioscorea edulis, D. alata,* and some others are natives of the East Indies, but having been early taken to the West Indies and other parts of tropical America, they are both cultivated and _naturalized. Their roots, often weighing thirty to forty pounds, are much used as food in those countries, and are occasionally seen in New York and other seaports, where they are esteemed by those who have lived in the countries where they are in use. The Chinese Yam is different from all other species of *Dioscorea* with edible roots, in being perfectly hardy in the Northern States, and it is vastly superior to the tropical yams in the edible quality of its root.

.The Chinese Yam is occasionally cultivated in the kitchen garden and truck patch, and is valued by many on account of its purity of flavor and the absence of any after taste of sweetness or other undesirable quality. The ease with which it can be cultivated and the facility with which it may be preserved also commend it. This yam was first sent to France, by a French consul, about the year 1849, from China, where it is in general cultivation. The plant was soon after sent to this country from the *Jardin des Plantes* at Paris, but it unfortunately fell into

56

the hands of an erratic nurseryman, who made such
extravagant claims as to its productiveness and value,
that those who tried it were greatly disappointed and
overlooked its real merits ; as a consequence, the Chinese
Yam fell into disrepute and became an object of ridicule.
The Chinese Yam has a root or tuber from eighteen inches
to three feet in length ; it is club-shaped, with the large
part below ; the portion near the surface of the ground is
not larger than the little finger, while the lower end is
two and sometimes three inches in diameter. The vine,
if furnished with a support, will grow to the hight of
twelve or fifteen feet, but is much shorter when allowed
to run upon the ground. The triangularly heart-shaped
leaves are about two inches long and of a dark glossy
green. The flowers are very minute, in small racemes in
the axils of the leaves ; they are dull yellow and are
pleasantly fragrant ; the plant is diœcious, only the male
or staminate form having been introduced, it bears no
fruit or seeds in this country. Large numbers of bulblets about the size of a large pea are produced in the
axils of the leaves ; as these grow readily and afford the
most common method of propagating the plant they are
usually sold by seedsmen.

It being very ornamental in its character the plant is
used to cover verandas, trellises, etc.; on account of the
fragrance of its flowers it is sometimes called and sold as
"The Cinnamon Vine."

As a field or garden crop it has never become popular,
mainly on account of the difficulty in harvesting. The
small end of the tuber is exceedingly brittle, and from
the fact that the large end is lowest, it can not be
pulled, but an excavation must be made to the full depth
to which it reaches. This difficulty may be obviated to
some extent by planting upon ridges.

Some persons who are exceedingly fond of the Chinese
yam, plant the roots in some convenient spot and, as they

are perfectly hardy, allow them to take care of themselves, digging them as they are needed. In cooking they may be treated in the same manner as potatoes. The bulblets do not produce a full-sized tuber the first year ; they may be sown in a seed-bed and the small tubers produced planted the next spring either whole or cut into two or three pieces, according to their size. When full-sized tubers are once obtained, their smaller ends are reserved for planting, using the large portion for the table ; these small ends are cut into lengths of one-and-a-half to three inches, according to their size, and will produce large tubers the first year. The distance in planting may be the same as for the Sweet Potato.

The tubers make their greatest increase in size late in the season, and should not be dug before frost has put an end to the growth of the vines.

CHAPTER XIX.

MANURING FOR SWEET POTATOES.—*Additional.*

The manures best adapted to the wants of the sweet potato are partially given in Chapter VI. of this work, but more special information is required, which is given here.

There is nothing much superior to well-rotted stable manure, applied in hills or drills. The superphosphates, bone meal, ammoniated bone, woods earth, wood ashes, potash, wood-pile and fence-corner scrapings, all give satisfactory results. Some cultivators apply from two to four hundred pounds of ammoniated superphosphate, containing potash, per acre. Others use old, decomposed, home-made manure, mixed with ashes and acid phosphate, in the open furrows or in the hills.

A correspondent in the "Southern Cultivator" desired to know: "What would be the cheapest—good stable manure that is hauled four miles, or cotton seed delivered on the farm at fifteen cents per bushel ? The stable manure costs twenty-five cents per ton." To which the editor replied : "The stable manure is the cheapest, if of good quality, and more likely to give satisfactory results. Rating the labor at fifty cents a day, and making two trips a day, a load or ton would cost fifty cents, exclusive of the use of team and wagon. The last item is a nominal one to a farmer, usually rated only as wear and tear. In this view of the case, a wagon load of manure would cost only a little more than three bushels of cotton seed—and, we would add, if well rotted, the stable manure would be to the crop double the value of the cotton seed."

When sweet potatoes are cultivated in new grounds of moderate depth of soil, very little if any fertilizers are required ; but, as a general rule cultivators find it pays best to give the plants proper food and enough of it.

W. B. McDaniel, of Georgia, says : "We have used Cumberland superphosphate at the rate of two hundred pounds per acre, and it doubled the yield, and made two hundred bushels without other fertilizers. We also obtained the same gratifying results from a brand of ammoniated bone."

CHAPTER XX.

PROPAGATING THE SWEET POTATO.—*Additional.*

In Chapter VII. of this work full directions will be found for preparing hot-beds for sweet potatoes, and for giving them a fair start.

How to Transplant Successfully.—As further information, we give the different views on this subject. Commissioner Henderson, of Georgia, gives Georgia farmers some excellent advice on transplanting. He thinks if farmers would cease to rely on the clouds for the moisture necessary to ensure the life of the transplanted slips, they would find no great difficulty in securing an early stand.

It is advised that the ground intended for potatoes should be kept in good tilth by repeated plowings, and when the slips are ready, set out at once. It is only necessary to have the ground freshly plowed. Strike off the crown of the ridge with a board or hoe ; set the plant in place and pour in a gill or half a pint of water, so as to wash the fine earth into the holes around the roots. This should be done late in the afternoon, and the next morning the wet soil and the partly filled holes may be covered with fine soil.

If the ground is not very dry the plant may be made to live by "grouting," which is simply dipping the roots of the plants into water in which a quantity of woods mold, clay soil, or fine cow manure has been stirred, and setting them without the further application of water. By adopting some such method, the plant beds, being freely watered after each drawing, will produce more abundantly and promptly, and the whole area intended for the crop may be set in good time.

SLIPS FOR LATE USE AND FOR SEED.—It is a good plan, if there be a suitable season in the latter part of June, to cut slips from the vines and set them in well-prepared ridges or hills. These, if well attended to, produce the late crop, and they answer very well for seed. This applies to Virginia and further south, and to various parts of the West. There is economy in this way of adding to the main crop.

CHAPTER XXI.

GENERAL REMARKS ON THE CULTURE AND MANAGEMENT OF THE SWEET POTATO.

The sweet potato is one of the most eatable and delicious of all esculents, and the regions adapted to its culture are quite extensive. It may be grown for family use, if not for market, as far north as Rochester, New York, and Lansing, Michigan, and in all the Southern and Southeastern States.

Sweet potatoes may be grown in a variety of soils, but that which is dry, warm and sandy will give the finest quality. If the land has a red cast, so much the better, think many farmers ; for this imparts the bright color to the roots that gains the good prices in market.

Deep plowing is not recommended for sweet potatoes. In deeply tilled soil the roots strike downward, and the result is long, spindling potatoes instead of short, compact ones. While the plowing should be shallow rather than deep, the ground must be thoroughly worked and sufficiently fertilized. Well decomposed stable manure is generally conceded to be the best fertilizer for this crop.

The ground should be warm and all danger from frost past before the plants are set out, but it is all the better for being prepared and marked off a little in advance of the season for transplanting. Growers in different sections differ in their opinions as to the merits of hill and row systems; good results have been gained from both, and the general impression appears to be that larger roots are obtained by the hill system, while cultivating in ridges produces the greatest number of potatoes. Most cultivators now mark off the ground and set the plants with a view to cultivating the crop by horse-power. If the plants are to be set in hills, three feet apart each way will be found a convenient distance; if to be cultivated in ridges, mark off the ground with a plow in rows about four feet apart. The ridges are usually made by throwing two furrows together over the manure that has been spread in a small furrow or marking for the row; then, with a hand-hoe, the ridges are smoothed and their tops patted down. When the time arrives for setting the plants, the crown of the ridge is pushed aside, one hand is thrust into the soil, while the other inserts the plants about sixteen inches apart in the rows. When the hill system is practiced, the rows are made into small hills with light hoes; the pointed tops of these hills are knocked off at the time of planting, so that the plants may be set in fresh earth. Some of our progressive farmers use long, slender, wooden tongs, in which the plant is held, to be inserted in the hole made with a wooden shovel in the other hand. These implements do away with the back-breaking business of setting the plants by hand in the ordinary way.

The ground should be moist at the time of planting; therefore, just previous to, or after, a rain is a favorable season. Growers generally agree that the roots of the plants ought to be wet; some water them, others prefer puddling or grouting the roots. From eight to ten thousand plants are required to set an acre. Row planting requires a larger number of plants than does hill culture.

About ten days or a fortnight after setting the plants, go over the ground and replant where for any reason the first setting has been destroyed ; cultivate during the summer and keep the ground free from weeds. Northern cultivators find it necessary to prevent the points of long vines from rooting down, for wherever those roots start a large number of potatoes will set. These (at the North) not only fail to gain a serviceable size, but they rob the hills of nutriment and productive power.

There are but few varieties of the sweet potato. Of these the Yellow and Red Nansemond are most extensively grown. The "Early Peabody" is favorably known to some of our Northern growers. The "Early Golden," a new early sweet potato, originated in Virginia, and a sport of the old "Early Red," is well spoken of by cultivators who have tried it. It is claimed that it is early, productive, and of pleasing quality. A well-known and much-cultivated sweet potato at the South is the "Yellow Yam ;" the "Pumpkin Yam" is also popular, though not so sweet as the first named. Other well-known sorts are "Hayti Yam" or "Musgrove ;" "Nigger Killer," a very prolific variety ; "Spanish Potato," and "Brazilian Yam." At the South there is no such thing as buying and selling potato plants. Farmers with one accord save their own seed. When they desire to plant slips

each man has his own plant bed. Sometimes the roots
are planted for an early patch the same as are Irish potatoes; then when the vines are fairly started they are
set out for a later crop. These vines doubled up and
stuck into the ground grow readily and bring, it is
thought by many, equally good results with those of seed
potatoes or slips.

Mr. Purdy says : "Parties as far north as Rochester,
New York, in planting sweet potatoes, will get much
the best and surest crops by not planting them on high
ridges. If so planted on soil nearly level, in this section,
they grow short and plump, and in a much shorter season
than when grown on high ridges. This practice came
from the South, and more especially sections where the
soil is light and thin, and the throwing up of ridges
essential to get good crops."

FLAT CULTURE.—This method, practised in sections
where the growing season is short, as recommended by
Mr. Purdy, may appear rather paradoxical, but he speaks
from experience. The sweet potato delights in light,
warm and dry soils. Level culture and short seasons do
not seem favorable to these conditions. Ridges and hills
are generally preferred in all the Southern potato regions.

CULTIVATION OF THE SWEET POTATO.—Although we
have already given different modes of culture, yet difference in latitude and seasons call for and require a more or
less varied treatment. This makes it proper that the
views and experience of cultivators in different regions
should be given, which should not perplex the reader, but
serve as a further guide to success, and aid in securing
the capabilities of his particular position and climate.

From the latter part of May to July first, in the climate of New York, the rooted sweet potato sprouts
should be transplanted to the field or garden. Break the
land thoroughly, but not necessarily deep ; low, level or

damp lands will not do ; high, dry, warm and mellow or loamy soils are best, and the fresher the better; new lands are always best. Lay off rows three and a half to four feet apart, and if convenient have them run north and south. In these furrows apply two to four hundred pounds per acre of ammoniated superphosphate, containing potash. If home-made manure is used, be sure that it is old and thoroughly decomposed, and if possible mix some wood ashes and acid phosphate with it. Cover this furrow by running on each side of it with a one-horse turn plow, thus making a narrow ridge, on which plant the slips eighteen inches apart ; keep clear of weeds and grass until the vines begin to run freely ; then hill up and lay by. It is better not to permit the vines to take root between the rows, as this will diminish the crop of large roots, and here they will not get large enough for use. Loosen up the vines occasionally. A prong-hoe is good for this purpose. Just before or directly after frost, dig the potatoes and store them away in a dry, warm place for winter and spring use.

THE IMPORTANCE OF THE SWEET POTATO AS AN ADJUNCT TO OTHER FARM CROPS.—The appreciation of the value and use of this desirable esculent seems to be rapidly on the increase. We predict for the sweet potato much more accurate knowledge of its range, nature and requisites in the future than has yet been attained. Doubtless a " boom " in the near future is at hand, and the sweet potato will be more generally cultivated and appreciated than ever before.

The sweet potato flourishes in light, sandy or loamy and warm soils, but it may be cultivated with advantage in almost any soil that will produce fair crops of Indian corn, tobacco or cotton ; but if the soil be light, with southern aspect, so much the better. It should be planted as early as frost will permit. Land on which corn will burn and dry up is just right for the sweet potato ; and if the season (after they have a good start) be ever so hot and dry, they will continue to grow as though it were ever so seasonable. The main point is to keep down the weeds and grass. If these get a start much labor, especially in hand weeding, will be necessary, and they are very impatient of disturbance in the hill or ridge, incident to close or careless weeding.

When the vines begin to run and take root in the balks or along the sides of the hills or ridges, they should be loosened from the soil with the hand or a pronged weeding hoe. This is also necessary in cultivation; and the pronged hoe is used to pull them out of the way of the plow. In harvesting, a two-horse plow is used to plow them out, the vines being cut off with a sharp weeding hoe or other implement. Then the roots are easily brought to the surface with the pronged hoe. Care should be taken that they are not bruised or broken. They are then carefully taken up, the soil shaken out, sorted, and placed in hampers or baskets. Boxes are best, as they get bruised in baskets. A spring wagon takes them to the place of storage or to market.

The special advantage of raising this crop is, that the dry, hot seasons (that with us of the South seem to be on the increase), are a requisite with the sweet potato. The dryer the season the larger and better the potato.

Let every farmer in Southern potato regions have his hot-bed ready by the first of April—north of Virginia it should be later—so as to be ready to plant by the 10th or 15th of May. What better or more desirable crop can he raise for home use, or even for home or distant markets?

HANOVER NOTES ON CULTIVATION.—We introduce here some excellent additional remarks on cultivation from the pen of Mr. J. W. Tinsley, an experienced sweet potato raiser from that celebrated potato region, Hanover County, Virginia:

"We usually try to set all we can in the month of

May. If set out after that time the crop is not generally remunerative. The proper soil is a light, sandy one, or any land that is well impregnated with sand. Stable manure is the best fertilizer; after that cow-pen manure. In this section, mold from the woods and pine tags are used in large quantities, the same land being often put in potatoes. I never have been able to make good sweet potatoes with guano or artificial fertilizers alone; but it is necessary to supply coarse manure of some kind to mix with it. My plan is, to drill in all the stable and cow-pen manure I can spare for my potatoes, and by that means it goes much farther. Three feet is the best distance for the rows to be apart, and I am accustomed to list on the manure that I have drilled in the rows, throwing up the list as high as I can with a single plow, putting two furrows together. I make it a rule never to list in a day more than I can set that day, as the plants live better in fresh soil. The distance for the plants in the row is twenty inches, and it is best to set them deep in the ground, for if they should be cut off by cut-worms or anything else, they will be more apt to come out again, and the roots get more of the moisture. The evening is the best time for setting out, after a moderate rain in May; if the moisture is sufficient you can usually set for four or five evenings. In June the sun is so hot it is very difficult to get plants to live without a good season. In the cultivation of potatoes the secret of success is never to let them get grassy, but work them as soon as a crust forms on the ground. If they get grassy it is impossible to remove the grass without injuring the potato roots; and it is easier to work them three times when there is no grass than once when they are grassy. You must always see that the hoes do not cut into the hill, but merely scrape the ground around the plant, and then pull up a little earth to it. Now, by my plan of horse cultivation I save a great deal of hoe work. First, throw out, in about ten days after setting out the plants, the little balk that was left in throwing up the list, and try to get the earth as high as you can on the list, so as to smother out any grass that might start to grow on the list where the potato plant is. Now, before this earth that I have thrown up by this plowing commences to put up grass, I run a cotton scraper, which is attached to Watts' A and B plow, as close as I can to the potato plants, throwing earth to them; try to not let it cut more than half an inch deep. A good plowman can run the point of the scraper within less than an inch of the potatoes. If the vines have run any, of course I have to send a man ahead to throw the vines into every alternate balk, and the scraper has to first run all through the patch on one side of the list and then have the vines thrown back to that side that has been worked and run on the other side. The last working with the plow is to throw all this earth the scraper pulled away from the list back to it, moving the vines out of the way just as was done for the scraper, and throwing on one side of the list all through the patch, and then come back and plow the other side in the same way, trying to make this fresh earth meet in the middle of the list. Let your hands come on behind and see that no vines are covered up, as nothing lessens the size of the potatoes in the ridge or hill more than to have the vines covered with soil."

The foregoing instructions on culture, by Mr. Tinsley, are so well adapted to a large portion of the potato regions, and are so plain and practical, that had we given nothing further on this subject cultivators with similar soils and in similar sections could hardly err in their management.

CHAPTER XXII.

MISCELLANEOUS VIEWS ON THE MANAGEMENT OF THE SWEET POTATO.

Of course on this subject, as on the culture and management of corn and tobacco, there must be various opinions, doubtless originating, in part, from difference in soil and climate. "We desire," says the "Rural Messenger," of Petersburg, Virginia, "only to touch on two or three points about which there is some diversity of practice, but points upon which a very large part of the success of potato culture depends.

"Setting Out.—First, as to the method of setting out the young plants or 'draws.' Most farmers wait for a shower to do this, believing there is no sort of show for potatoes put out in dry weather. This is a mistake. Besides losing time, which is an important item in this crop, the 'draws' seldom grow off as well after a shower, especially if the soil hardens rapidly, and very often they remain for several days, sometimes more than a week, in a yellow, sickly state, and perhaps after all many of them die. Now, it is always best to plant everything in a freshly stirred soil. And if, when the bed has a goodly number of 'draws' fit to set, the ridges are thrown up, and little holes made the proper distance apart for setting sweet potatoes (fifteen inches), a plant put in each hole, and a little water poured in upon the roots, and after the water has all soaked into the soil the dry earth is drawn up to the plant, very few of them will die. In this way you plant in a freshly stirred soil, the ridge or hill is moist all through and loose and mellow, the pouring on of the water settles the roots into the soil and gives the plant moisture enough to start it into growth, and the drawing up of the dry soil around the plant prevents the part that is wet from getting hard. If the work is done late in the afternoon, nearly every plant will live, even in the dryest weather.

"ABOUT SEED.—There has lately arisen some difference of practice. Instead of cutting vines and sticking them out into ridges, in August, to make small seed potatoes, many now select the small roots from the large potatoes at digging time and use these for seed. It is noticed, however, by some, that the number of beds that fail to give an early supply of plants is increasing. Hotbeds are made with all due care, slips or small potatoes are bedded now as formerly, and all is done that can be thought of to insure a full show of early plants. But very often it is high June before a single drawing is secured. What is the cause? It must be the seed. Little potatoes for the general crop are not the best. They are dwarfs and late. Young slips, fresh and vigorous, are the best. These come from good-sized potatoes. Such sprout sooner in the bed and send up more of them. If you want early and fine potatoes, free from disease and true to kind, raise from potatoes of the vine you wish to grow. Potatoes will 'mix in the hill' if you plant more than one kind in a patch.

"It would seem but a trifling thing, but our experience is, that rows running north and south yield better than rows running east and west. It may be because the ridges or hills receive an equal amount of heat on both sides. We do not know. A free exposure to sun and air is also essential. The potato will not grow in the shade.

"EARLY VARIETIES.—As to earliness, we have found the 'White Yam' the earliest, but not the best. It is, however, a fine potato, and very prolific. Some call it the 'Harman,' but others claim that they are distinct varieties. The 'Red Yam' is, *par excellence,* the potato

in every essential point—earliness, quality and yield per
acre. The ' Yellow Rind' is hardy, prolific and good—
a fine general utility potato, good for table, stock, or
market; also, a good keeper. A large part of every
farmer's patch should be of this variety.

"Should the young plants look yellow and weakly
some time after being set, a sprinkling of plaster will re-
store them. But for small patches, where you are trying
to have a few very early, the best thing is liquid manure
made from stable or barn-yard manure. This should be
sprinkled around the plants every day or two, for some
days after planting."

HARVESTING.—The New York "Farmer's World" has
this to say about sweet potatoes : " There are few crops
more susceptible to injury by cold and frost than sweet
potatoes ; hence, sweet potatoes must be harvested before
the weather is sufficiently cold to freeze the ground. In
a word, sweet potatoes ought to be lifted from the ground
as soon as they are ripe. Care must be exercised not to
harvest them, however, until quite matured ; for unripe
roots will not keep. A good test is breaking open the
potato ; if ripe it maintains its light color when broken ;
if still immature, it will exude a gummy juice and turn
dark as it dries. There are growers who do not harvest
their sweet potatoes just at the period of mature growth
and before the the frost has touched the vines, but delay
until the vines are killed. This practice cannot be called
a safe one, for while slight frosts do not, in many cases,
injure the potatoes, it frequently occurs that when they
are left in the ground until the vines are destroyed they
come out with frosted ends, and the consequence is an
ill-flavored and bitter root when cooked.

"Like Irish potatoes, sweet potatoes should by all means
be lifted in dry weather. Sweet potatoes may be rapidly
harvested with the plow. Once out of the ground, they

must be air-dried in the shade previous to storing in winter quarters.

"Small quantities in this locality may be kept for home consumption, up to January 1st, by packing in boxes or barrels in alternate layers of leaves or kiln-dried sand or any earth. Large growers at the North build regular potato or root houses for the preservation of the sweet potato, with suitable arrangements for maintaining the proper degree of heat. In these houses the potatoes are packed in dry sand in bins."

SWEET POTATO PLANT-BEDS.—Mr. A. B. Cook, of Chesterfield County, Virginia, gives the following as his mode of making sweet potato hot-beds : "Have the pit in a well-drained place. First place green pine boughs or twigs and trample close until about six inches in depth ; then thoroughly wet. On this three or four inches of well-packed stable manure. Then place three or four inches of good, rich soil and rake smooth. Bed the potatoes, pressing or firming each potato in the soil ; cover with about three inches of woods mold or fine sand. Repeated experiments on a large scale have convinced me that the soundness and good size of the seed potato is the only necessary test."

HOT-BEDS.—Mr. Luther R. Bailey, Jarratt's Depot, Sussex County, Virginia, gives his mode of constructing hot-beds : "The *modus operandi* in this sweet potato country is as follows : I select a good, warm spot in my garden, with southern exposure, and dig out a pit twelve inches deep, and in length and width according to the quantity I wish to bed. Then fill the pit nearly to the top with dry stable manure ; then throw on earth to the depth of six inches ; smooth this and place on the potatoes evenly, but do not let them touch. Then cover with earth about four inches deep. By the first of May the sets will be up, and some large enough to draw.

Select a light and not too rich soil for your patch. We plant three and a half feet apart and use good, well-rotted stable manure in the ridges."

THE SWEET POTATO AS FOOD FOR STOCK.—A writer from Monteith, North Carolina, says : " Many farmers fail to properly value the sweet potato as a food crop. It makes fine feed for all kinds of stock. Hogs improve rapidly upon them, and I have found nothing to excel them as a food for producing milk and butter. The yield per acre is so abundant, it seems a little strange that more attention is not given to their culture. An average crop, for my section of the State, is about three hundred and fifty bushels. Farmers who give good attention to this crop will greatly reduce their expenses in the way of food."

PROPER TIME FOR HARVESTING.—This is very important. J. V. Dansby, of Pensacola, Florida, says : " Potatoes should be harvested as soon as they are ripe. At that time the leaves assume a yellow hue, and the roots, after being cut and exposed to the sun and air, appear white ; should there be upon the cut surface a green tinge the potato is not ripe. Do not wait for a frost before beginning to gather." Mr. D. also gives valuable instructions as to keeping large quantities. He has them to come out " bright and sound " late in the spring.

CUTTINGS VS. SETS OR PLANTS.—A Floyd County, Georgia, correspondent of the "Southern Cultivator," says : " We begin to set out plants in May, and continue until July, when we substitute cuttings from the vines. These we set through July, sometimes as late as the 10th of August, as we intend these to make our seed potatoes, though we often get many fine eating potatoes from these cuttings. In 1882 we set out a patch of little less than an acre of these cuttings on the 18th of July. They were plowed and hoed once each, and harvested

125 bushels, more than half of them marketable potatoes.

"KEEPING SWEET POTATOES IN EARTH.—I see in the March number of 'The Cultivator' a premium offered for the best plan for preserving sweet potatoes. I do not desire the premium, but will simply give your readers my experience in a few words.

"Just as soon as the frost has touched the vines I go to digging, and if possible carry them to the cellar as fast as plowed out, as the cellar is the only safe place to keep them in in this climate. When I begin to pour down, I also commence to throw dry earth over them to absorb the sweat, and continue this until the potatoes are all in. I put nothing else over them until the weather turns freezing cold, when I throw more earth over them until they are covered up entirely. A few inches of this covering will suffice. In this condition I let them remain until spring. I have made this a matter of study, and have decided that it is the potato's nature to both grow and remain in earth." The above are the views of Mr. D. D. Fleming, of Sterling, Alabama. In a good, dry cellar doubtless there could be no better plan than "keeping in earth." The covering, we think, should be increased in quite cold weather. Mr. W. A. Sanford, Beech Bluff, Tennessee, also uses dry earth in a dry cellar: "I keep them from one planting to another. They keep sound all the year."

CHAPTER XXIII.

THE HILL AND ROW SYSTEMS.

Cultivators in different sections differ in their opinions as to the merits of the hill and row systems. Good results are obtained from both, and the general impression appears to be that larger roots are obtained by the hill system, while cultivating in ridges produces the greatest number of potatoes. Most cultivators now-a-days mark off the ground and set the plants with a view to cultivating the crop by horse-power. If the plants are to be set in hills, three feet apart each way will be found a convenient distance; if to be cultivated in ridges, mark off the ground with the plow in rows about four feet apart. The ridges are conveniently made by throwing two furrows together over the manure that has been spread in a furrow or marking for the row; then with a hand hoe the ridges are smoothed and their tops patted down. When the time comes for setting the plants, the dry tops of the ridges are removed and the plants set from sixteen to eighteen inches apart in the row. In large fields the crowns of the ridges are taken off with a light scraper, drawn by a horse, and wide enough to do two rows at a time.

When the hill system is practised these rows are usually made into small hills with light hoes. The points of these hills are knocked off at the time of planting, so that the plants may be set in fresh, moist earth.

After the land is well prepared it is laid off into rows about three or three and a half feet apart with a single-horse turn-plow; then a furrow is thrown up each side of these rows each way, as in hilling for tobacco. It is now light work to form hills with the weeding-hoe.

If the soil requires food, they run a furrow each way as above, and at the intersection of the rows a shovelful of manure is put in the places. The manure is sometimes fine woods earth mixed with ashes, or, if this cannot be had, any rich soil well mixed with stable manure is employed. The manure being in place, the loose soil around is pulled up with the weeding-hoe, so as to form a hill on the manure. When ready to plant, the tops of these hills are cut off with a weeding-hoe, and the plants are set in the center of these flattened tops. It is claimed for this mode that it requires less labor, and some farmers think produces larger crops. The after culture, it is said, is also less difficult.

The ground should be moist at the time of planting. Therefore, just after a moderate rain is a favorable season. The roots of the plants at time of setting, at all events, must be wet. Therefore, puddling should be resorted to when planting time comes without showery weather.

CHAPTER XXIV.

THE VALUE OF THE SWEET POTATO.

The editor of the "Charleston News" gives his estimate of the sweet potato and his views as to the future of this most eatable, delicious and valuable of all root crops as follows. He says: " We have always been of opinion that the great value of the sweet potato crop in the Southern States and elsewhere was not duly appreciated and sufficiently utilized. Root crops are always more prolific than grain crops. They exhaust the land less and give more in return for labor and manure. Of course they are not as nutritious, pound for pound, as grain, but in great increase of material they yield more nutrition to a given quantity of land, than any of the cereals. Irish potatoes, turnips, beets, carrots, both in Europe and in our Northern States, are all justly prized as the most valuable of farm crops. The sweet potato is superior to them all as food for man and beast. It may be used for all the purposes to which the others are applied and for many others besides. In the fresh state, just out of the ground, it makes an excellent substitute for arrowroot by grating the pulp into water and allowing the starchy matter to subside.

"As a vegetable it is a favorite on every table, cooked in great variety of ways. As a dessert, it makes better pudding or pie than the pumpkin. It is good food for stock of all kinds—horses, cattle, sheep and hogs. We knew an old planter once who always raised an abundance of corn and other provisions for his stock, but who was an enthusiast over the sweet potato crop, estimating it on the yield returned from the labor bestowed as of more value than any other food producing crop.

"Our best Southern varieties will probably soon become a very important article of export to the Northern States and to Europe. The farmers in Georgia are complaining that with an immense crop of favorite 'Yellow Yam,' raised in expectation of shipment, there is no demand in the Northern market for the variety, the Northern people preferring the dryer sorts.

"We have ourselves been noticing this thing for some time with a good deal of surprise. In the St. Louis prices current sent us, the 'Southern Queen' ('Poplar root') and 'Red Bermuda' ('Musgrove'), two of our worst varieties, are each quoted at about double the price set upon the 'Yellow Yam.'" Our contemporary says it is because they don't know how to cook the Yam up there, and adds: "A well-seasoned 'Yam,' baked slowly, as it should be, is really more a fruit than a

vegetable. The time will come when they will be prepared in this way, and, by being put up in sealed cans
and by other modes of conveyance, will become an important article of trade to the North as well as to Europe." They are putting up cans already in some parts
of the country.

CHAPTER XXV.

HOW TO SAVE SWEET POTATOES.

We gather the following excellent and practical views
from the "Southern Cultivator and Dixie Farmer:"

"The inquiries about saving sweet potatoes, and the
many designs for potato-houses, induce me to give you a
practical, and, at the same time, a most economical plan
for this purpose. The old-fashioned, slipshod way of
digging and putting up potatoes, so common with a
large class of our planters, is a mockery, and especially
do we find it so, for season after season the same hack-
neyed phrase greets us: 'My potatoes all rotted this
year. How did yours keep?' Yet the majority of
them will try the same plan, year after year, without in-
quiring the reason. Few men know when to dig potatoes, and quite a number of failures may be attributed
to this cause. No farmer will gather his corn until
fully ripe. Just so he should act in saving his potatoes. Potatoes should be dug when fully ripe, whether
the vines have been nipped by a slight frost or not; but
as a general rule, it is best, or as well, for a slight frost
to nip the vines before digging should occur. To ascer-
tain when to dig and put up potatoes a few should be
selected and cut or split open. If the cuts dry white,
dig; but should they dry dark, let them stand a **few**

days. Potatoes ripen rapidly at this season of the year, and nothing is lost by delay, unless there be danger of a killing frost.

"To understand fully the plan of saving potatoes it is necessary to commence with the house; and by this we do not mean a building made tight to preserve the potatoes, but merely a house to keep the sand, dust or earth dry and to keep out rogues. The one used at my father's is a log cabin, with an earthen floor covered to the depth of two feet (less, we think, would do), with dry sand, dust or earth. When the potatoes are dug move them and pile up in the corners of the house, to remain in this condition until they go through a sweat. The time occupied in this process depends largely on the state of the weather. Should the weather become cool sufficiently to chill the potatoes, a little straw or leaves should be placed over them, and a little sand, dust or dry earth also when the sweating is through with. Then commence to put away for future use by emptying a basketful in the center of the house and throwing over this pile a few shovelfuls of dry material (sand is best). Continue this until all the potatoes are put into this big heap and covered to the depth of two or three inches with one of the materials above mentioned. Should a rogue break into your heap, or the covering be neglected, only those exposed to the weather will spoil. You can go into the bank without any danger, and you can rest assured that your potatoes will keep from year to year.

"The final covering may be two or three inches when first put away, but as the weather grows cold (especially as applied to colder sections), this, doubtless, we think, should be increased to an extent sufficient to secure the potatoes from cold or freezing."

CHAPTER XXVI.

HARVESTING AND STORING SWEET POTATOES.

A correspondent from Wisconsin makes the following statement : "I raise a good many sweet potatoes, and have kept them perfectly sound through winter by digging promptly after the vines are frosted (we and others say, dig sweet potatoes before the frost kills the vines) ; spread thinly in an airy, dry place, where they will not be chilled, leaving them for a couple of weeks, or until they are perceptibly wilted ; then wrap all those which are an inch through or upward in papers, and pack them snugly in barrels, and place them up stairs, near a chimney, in a room where it does not freeze. The small potatoes I pack in sand which has been dried in a kiln or oven, and set them in a similar place."

Mr. J. B. Wallace, of Chico, Wise Country, Texas, gives his mode of keeping and storing sweet potatoes as follows : "I think the most essential thing is to dig them at the proper time, and I think that time is about the full moon in October—that is, in Texas. No matter about the weather, unless the ground is too wet. I never wait for frost ; but if frost comes before the full moon, dig as soon possible, or at least before any rain. I dig with a bull-tongue plow ; but any way will do, if they are not cut or bruised. In gathering them, sort out the cut ones, but before putting up let them have at least one day's sun ; if the ground is wet, two days or more is better, but in no case let them take the dew at night. I put them in a shallow cellar, say from three to four feet deep, under some house. After they are put away, throw a little fine, dry earth over them—just enough to dust over the cut potatoes, if there be any. This will cause them to dry and not commence rotting. Let them lie that way till the weather begins to turn cool ; then cover up as the weather gets colder, until they are covered from ten to twelve inches deep. In all cases cover with dry earth. I differ with those who want straw or leaves under potatoes; I want them on the ground, where they will keep plump and sound, and the protection from frost will be equally good.

"When they are bulked or pitted out of doors they should be on an elevated place, or throw up the earth so that water will not stand about them. Place the potatoes on the naked ground—about thirty or forty bushels in a bulk; set up corn stalks or similar material around them; then spread some dry grass or leaves on top, and bank up enough soil to this covering to hold it on. Let them stand that way till the weather begins to get cool; then commence to cover deeper. When the weather becomes very cold they should be covered with soil to the depth of at least twelve or fifteen inches, but in warmer weather they should have a little air at the top. In all cases have them well sheltered; a very small leak will ruin a bulk of potatoes. This is my experience of twenty years in Texas."

We endorse most of the above directions. Doubtless, for the climate of Texas, the plan of Mr. Wallace works well. Perhaps in colder regions deeper covering and protection from extreme cold would be necessary. It is not probable that Mr. Wallace attaches any importance to the "sign" of the moon, but gives the "full moon" in October as a suitable average time for his locality.

It is always best to dig sweet potatoes before the frost kills the vines. Select, if possible, a dry time for this work, and, in storing for home use or for market, we repeat, be sure the potatoes are as free from moisture as possible. No vegetable will rot sooner from dampness or wet than the sweet potato. Attend to this; secure them from freezing and they are generally safe.

H. M. Minster gives the following directions for keeping sweet potatoes. His mode, doubtless, is good, especially for saving them for home use ; and we believe, as he says, they may be kept from year to year in those warm newspaper beds, even without being near the stove pipe, in some Southern sections. It might not be practicable or convenient to adopt this plan where large quantities are raised for market. He says : "I give my mode for saving sweet potatoes. I have a dry goods box which holds twelve or fifteen bushels of potatoes. I set this box against the stove pipe up stairs. Line the box inside —bottom, sides and ends—to the top with twelve to fifteen thicknesses of newspapers, carefully breaking the joints. The box is now ready for the potatoes. Dig them when ripe, and before they get injured with cold in the patch, take them up stairs. You can let them lay a few days before placing them in the box, or put them in as you take them up if they are dry. Do not put anything on top of the potatoes except the lid of the box, and that must not fit tight until cold weather. You can easily tell if the lid is too close, as the potatoes will sweat, and moisture gather on the under side of the lid and even on the potatoes. I have kept sweet potatoes in this way perfectly sound from year to year. They are so fine when other vegetables are scarce ; they can be cooked in various ways, and everybody likes them."

CHAPTER XXVII.

SWEET POTATOES IN NORTHERN LOCALITIES.

SWEET POTATOES IN OHIO.—"I believe sweet potatoes can be profitably grown much farther North than is generally supposed, or wherever any variety of corn will ripen," says Mr. W. M. Rathbone, Marietta, Ohio, who has made the sweet potato crop a study for years. Mr. Rathbone plants in ridges three feet apart from center to center, with the plants set in the ridge eighteen to twenty-four inches apart. After every shower that forms a crust, he ploughs lightly with a three-shovel plough constructed especially for the work, and scrapes down the crust and incipient weeds—do not let these get a fair start—with the two small shovels on the outer shafts, while the large shovel attached behind to a center-beam heaves the ridges up again, all in one performance. As soon as the vines cover the ground he is ready for a drouth, which injures this crop less than any other.

Most people, in Mr. Rathbone's opinion, err in selecting land that is too wet for the sweet potato crop. They also plant too close. In New York, Maine or Canada, Mr. R. suggests that the hills on these soils ought to be as far apart as those of corn, in order to insure ample sunlight as the crop approaches maturity.

SWEET POTATOES IN ONTARIO, CANADA.—Few persons have an idea of the wide range of the sweet potato, and would hardly expect that fine, large potatoes could be raised in the Province of Ontario, Canada; but such is the fact. We have before us a report of the "Fruit Growers' Association of the Province of Ontario," from which we glean the following :

" 'Yellow Nansemond' is probably one of the best varieties for this Province ; succeeds well, very prolific, and often grows as large as six pounds in weight. 'Bermuda' is a fine flavored variety, but appears to require a longer season to reach perfection than the other. It is not so prolific or so sure a cropper. 'Early Peabody:' A white potato, smaller in size than either of the above, and not so prolific, but of good quality.

"There are several other varieties, but, after testing, these three, in the order given, are considered as the best. The only difficulty to contend with is, to get a long enough season to bring them to perfection—to get out the plants as early as possible, but not so early as to endanger them by frost."

Full directions follow for planting and culture, which we omit, as they are similar to those practiced in our Northern States.

CHAPTER XXVIII.

COOKING SWEET POTATOES.

As an article of diet the sweet potato is justly considered a luxury and the most delicious of all esculents. It can be cooked in various ways, with less condiments and less trouble than any other production of the garden or field.

LITTLE'S METHOD.—"Little," of Belton, Texas, tells "The Housekeeper" her plan for cooking sweet potatoes: "Wash them in a pan, pouring a little hot water over them; set in an oven to bake, turning them so as to bake evenly; pour in more water as needed; let the pan be about dry when they get done; place on a dish and serve; or halve them—if very large, quarter them—first peeling, and bake in a pan with roast beef or fresh pork, basting them often with the drippings. They will be found very nice."

SWEET POTATO PIE.—The following recipe for sweet potato pie comes all the way from Arkansas : "One quart of sweet potatoes boiled and well strained, three beaten eggs, three tablespoonfuls of sugar, one tablespoonful of butter, half a nutmeg (grated), half a teaspoonful of ground cinnamon, a little ground cloves, a little lemon peel, or a little essence of lemon, enough cream or milk to make the mixture of the consistency of batter ; make a rich pastry, and, covering your bake-plate, pour in the mixture and bake with a top crust." The above must make a rich pie, wholesome and appetizing. Half the condiments might be omitted, and still it would be most excellent.

GLAZED SWEET POTATOES.—Boil softly, peel carefully, and lay in a greased dripping-pan in a good oven. As they begin to crust over, baste with a little butter, repeating this several times as they brown. When glossy and of a golden russet color, serve.

SWEET POTATO PUDDING.—Two coffee-cupfuls of mashed, boiled sweet potatoes ; add one teacupful of sugar, one teacupful of butter, four eggs, one teacupful of sweet cream, one teaspoonful of cinnamon, one grated nutmeg, one teaspoonful of extract of lemon, and a pinch of soda dissolved in a teaspoonful of water. Beat the eggs light ; add sugar and butter rubbed to a cream ; stir all together with the mashed potatoes while hot. Cover a deep plate with puff paste ; pour in the mixture. Bake in a moderate oven. When done, cover the top with slices of fruit marmalade and sprinkle thickly with granulated sugar.

CHAPTER XXIX.

SWEET POTATOES FOR HOGS.

The propagation and culture of the sweet potato are especially profitable and cheap. No difficulty in raising the crop, but its keeping requires care and attention. Farmers in the South who are not convenient to markets, and who are not prepared for storing or do not care to winter the crop, would doubtless do well to use the surplus product as food for hogs.

"Every farmer in the sweet potato regions," says Mr. W. L. Jones, of the "Southern Cultivator," "ought to plant largely of the San Domingo type of sweet potatoes for fattening hogs in the fall. Considering quality and quantity, we know of no other food so easily and cheaply raised for this purpose. If the potatoes and corn are dried at the temperature of boiling water, three bushels of potatoes will contain as much dry matter as one of corn—not as much fat or albuminous matter in proportion as corn, but more of the starch group of constituents than corn. Peas would make up the deficiency in the potato admirably. The two would fit well together and make almost a perfect ration for fattening hogs. Have a potato and pea patch in the same enclosure, so that the hogs may eat of each at will, and you have the foundation for cheap pork."

STANDARD BOOKS.

Forest Planting.

By H. NICHOLAS JARCHOW, LL. D. A treatise on the care of woodlands and the restoration of the denuded timberlands on plains and mountains. The author has fully described those European methods which have proved to be most useful in maintaining the superb forests of the old world. This experience has been adapted to the different climates and trees of America, full instructions being given for forest planting of our various kinds of soil and subsoil, whether on mountain or valley. Illustrated. 250 pages. 5x7 inches. Cloth. $1.50

Soils and Crops of the Farm.

By GEORGE E. MORROW, M. A., and THOMAS F. HUNT. The methods of making available the plant food in the soil are described in popular language. A short history of each of the farm crops is accompanied by a discussion of its culture. The useful discoveries of science are explained as applied in the most approved methods of culture. Illustrated. 310 pages. 5x7 inches. Cloth. $1.00

Land Draining.

A handbook for farmers on the principles and practice of draining, by MANLY MILES, giving the results of his extended experience in laying tile drains. The directions for the laying out and the construction of tile drains will enable the farmer to avoid the errors of imperfect construction, and the disappointment that must necessarily follow. This manual for practical farmers will also be found convenient for reference in regard to many questions that may arise in crop growing, aside from the special subjects of drainage of which it treats. Illustrated. 200 pages. 5x7 inches. Cloth. . . $1.00

Barn Plans and Outbuildings.

Two hundred and fifty-seven illustrations. A most valuable work, full of ideas, hints, suggestions, plans, etc., for the construction of barns and outbuildings, by practical writers. Chapters are devoted to the economic erection and use of barns, grain barns, horse barns, cattle barns, sheep barns, cornhouses, smokehouses, icehouses, pig pens, granaries, etc. There are likewise chapters on birdhouses, doghouses, tool sheds, ventilators, roofs and roofing, doors and fastenings, workshops, poultry houses, manure sheds, barnyards, root pits, etc. 235 pages. 5x7 inches. Cloth. . . . $1.00

1

Herbert's Hints to Horse Keepers.

By the late HENRY WILLIAM HERBERT (Frank Forester). This is one of the best and most popular works on the horse prepared in this country. A complete manual for horsemen, embracing: How to breed a horse; how to buy a horse; how to break a horse; how to use a horse; how to feed a horse; how to physic a horse (allopathy or homeopathy); how to groom a horse; how to drive a horse; how to ride a horse, etc. Beautifully illustrated. 425 pages. 5x7 inches. Cloth. $1.50

Diseases of Horses and Cattle.

By DR. D. McINTOSH, V. S., professor of veterinary science in the university of Illinois. Written expressly for the farmer, stockman and veterinary student. A new work on the treatment of animal diseases, according to the modern status of veterinary science, has become a necessity. Such an one is this volume of over 400 pages, written by one of the most eminent veterinarians of our country. Illustrated. 426 pages. 5x7 inches. Cloth. $1.75

The Ice Crop.

By THERON L. HILES. How to harvest, ship and use ice. A complete, practical treatise for farmers, dairymen, ice dealers, produce shippers, meat packers, cold storers, and all interested in icehouses, cold storage, and the handling or use of ice in any way. Including many recipes for iced dishes and beverages. The book is illustrated by cuts of the tools and machinery used in cutting and storing ice, and the different forms of icehouses and cold storage buildings. Illustrated. 122 pages. 5x7 inches. Cloth. $1.00

The Secrets of Health, or How Not to Be Sick, and How to Get Well from Sickness.

By S. H. PLATT, A. M., M. D., late member of the Connecticut Eclectic Medical Society, the National Eclectic Medical Association, and honorary member of the National Bacteriological Society of America; our medical editor and author of "Talks With Our Doctor" and "Our Health Adviser." Nearly 600 pages. An index of 20 pages, so that any topic may be instantly consulted. A new departure in medical knowledge for the people—the latest progress, secrets and practices of all schools of healing made available for the common people—health without medicine, nature without humbug, common sense without folly, science without fraud. 81 illustrations. 576 pages. 5x7 inches. Cloth. $1.50

STANDARD BOOKS.

Hunter and Trapper.

By HALSEY THRASHER, an old and experienced sportsman. The best modes of hunting and trapping are fully explained, and foxes, deer, bears, etc., fall into his traps readily by following his directions. Illustrated. 92 pages. 5x7 inches. Cloth. $0.50

Batty's Practical Taxidermy and Home Decoration.

By JOSEPH H. BATTY, taxidermist for the government surveys and many colleges and museums in the United States. An entirely new and complete as well as authentic work on taxidermy—giving in detail full directions for collecting and mounting animals, birds, reptiles, fish, insects, and general objects of natural history. 125 illustrations. 204 pages. 5x7 inches. Cloth. $1.00

Hemp.

By S. S. BOYCE. A practical treatise on the culture of hemp for seed and fiber, with a sketch of the history and nature of the hemp plant. The various chapters are devoted to the soil and climate adapted to the culture of hemp for seed and for fiber, irrigating, harvesting, retting and machinery for handling hemp. Illustrated. 112 pages. 5x7 inches. Cloth. $0.50

Alfalfa.

By F. D. COBURN. Its growth, uses and feeding value. The fact that alfalfa thrives in almost any soil; that without reseeding, it goes on yielding two, three, four and sometimes five cuttings annually for five, ten, or perhaps 100 years; and that either green or cured it is one of the most nutritious forage plants known, makes reliable information upon its production and uses of unusual interest. Such information is given in this volume for every part of America, by the highest authority. Illustrated. 164 pages. 5x7 inches. Cloth. $0.50

Talks on Manure.

By JOSEPH HARRIS, M. S. A series of familiar and practical talks between the author and the deacon, the doctor, and other neighbors, on the whole subject of manures and fertilizers; including a chapter especially written for it by Sir John Bennet Lawes of Rothamsted, England. 366 pages. 5x7 inches. Cloth. $1.50

STANDARD BOOKS.

Practical Forestry.

By Andrew S. Fuller. A treatise on the propagation, planting and cultivation, with descriptions and the botanical and popular names of all the indigenous trees of the United States, and notes on a large number of the most valuable exotic species. Illustrated. 300 pages. 5x7 inches. Cloth. $1.50

Irrigation for the Farm, Garden and Orchard.

By Henry Stewart. This work is offered to those American farmers and other cultivators of the soil who, from painful experience, can readily appreciate the losses which result from the scarcity of water at critical periods. Fully illustrated. 276 pages. 5x7 inches. Cloth. . . $1.00

Irrigation Farming.

By Lute Wilcox. A handbook for the practical application of water in the production of crops. A complete treatise on water supply, canal construction, reservoirs and ponds, pipes for irrigation purposes, flumes and their structure, methods of applying water, irrigation of field crops, the garden, the orchard and vineyard, windmills and pumps, appliances and contrivances. New edition, revised, enlarged and rewritten. Profusely illustrated. Over 500 pages. 5x7 inches. Cloth. $2.00

Ginseng, Its Cultivation, Harvesting, Marketing and Market Value.

By Maurice G. Kains, with a short account of its history and botany. It discusses in a practical way how to begin with either seed or roots, soil, climate and location, preparation, planting and maintenance of the beds, artificial propagation, manures, enemies, selection for market and for improvement, preparation for sale, and the profits that may be expected. This booklet is concisely written, well and profusely illustrated, and should be in the hands of all who expect to grow this drug to supply the export trade, and to add a new and profitable industry to their farms and gardens, without interfering with the regular work. New edition. Revised and enlarged. Illustrated. 5x7 inches. Cloth. . . . $0.50

Truck Farming at the South.

By A. Oemler. A work giving the experience of a successful grower of vegetables or "garden truck" for northern markets. Essential to anyone who contemplates entering this profitable field of agriculture. Illustrated. 274 pages. 5x7 inches. Cloth. $1.00

4

Henderson's Practical Floriculture.

By PETER HENDERSON. A guide to the successful propagation and cultivation of florists' plants. The work is not one for florists and gardeners only, but the amateur's wants are constantly kept in mind, and we have a very complete treatise on the cultivation of flowers under glass, or in the open air, suited to those who grow flowers for pleasure as well as those who make them a matter of trade. New and enlarged edition. Beautifully illustrated. 325 pages. 5x7 inches. Cloth. $1.50

Mushrooms. How to Grow Them.

By WILLIAM FALCONER. This is the most practical work on the subject ever written, and the only book on growing mushrooms published in America. The author describes how he grows mushrooms, and how they are grown for profit by the leading market gardeners, and for home use by the most successful private growers. Engravings drawn from nature expressly for this work. 170 pages. 5x7 inches. Cloth. $1.00

Play and Profit in My Garden.

By E. P. ROE. The author takes us to his garden on the rocky hillsides in the vicinity of West Point, and shows us how out of it, after four years' experience, he evoked a profit of $1000. and this while carrying on pastoral and literary labor. It is very rarely that so much literary taste and skill are mated to so much agricultural experience and good sense. Illustrated. 350 pages. 5x7 inches. Cloth. . . $1.00

Fumigation Methods.

By WILLIS G. JOHNSON. A timely up-to-date book on the practical application of the new methods for destroying insects with hydrocyanic acid gas and carbon bisulphid, the most powerful insecticides ever discovered. It is an indispensable book for farmers, fruit growers, nurserymen, gardeners, florists, millers, grain dealers, transportation companies, college and experiment station workers, etc. Illustrated. 313 pages. 5x7 inches. Cloth. $1.00

Fungi and Fungicides.

By PROF. CLARENCE M. WEED. A practical manual concerning the fungous diseases of cultivated plants and the means of preventing their ravages. The author has endeavored to give such a concise account of the most important facts relating to these as will enable the cultivator to combat them intelligently. 90 illustrations. 222 pages. 5x7 inches. Paper, 50 cents; cloth $1.00

STANDARD BOOKS.

Insects and Insecticides.

By CLARENCE M. WEED, D. Sc., professor of entomology and zoology, New Hampshire college of agriculture. A practical manual concerning noxious insects, and methods of preventing their injuries. Many illustrations. 334 pages. 5x7 inches. Cloth. $1.50

How Crops Grow.

By PROF. SAMUEL W. JOHNSON of Yale college. New and revised edition. A treatise on the chemical composition, structure and life of the plant. This book is a guide to the knowledge of agricultural plants, their composition, their structure and modes of development and growth; of the complex organization of plants, and the use of the parts; the germination of seeds, and the food of plants obtained both from the air and the soil. The book is indispensable to all real students of agriculture. With numerous illustrations and tables of analysis. 416 pages. 5x7 inches. Cloth. $1.50

Tobacco Leaf.

By J. B. KILLEBREW and HERBERT MYRICK. Its Culture and Cure, Marketing and Manufacture. A practical handbook on the most approved methods in growing, harvesting, curing, packing and selling tobacco, with an account of the operations in every department of tobacco manufacture. The contents of this book are based on actual experiments in field, curing barn, packing house, factory and laboratory. It is the only work of the kind in existence, and is destined to be the standard practical and scientific authority on the whole subject of tobacco for many years. 506 pages and 150 original engravings. 5x7 inches. Cloth. $2.00

Coburn's Swine Husbandry.

By F. D. COBURN. New, revised and enlarged edition. The breeding, rearing and management of swine, and the prevention and treatment of their diseases. It is the fullest and freshest compendium relating to swine breeding yet offered. Illustrated. 312 pages. 5x7 inches. Cloth. $1.50

Home Pork Making.

The art of raising and curing pork on the farm. By A. W. FULTON. A complete guide for the farmer, the country butcher and the suburban dweller, in all that pertains to hog slaughtering, curing, preserving and storing pork product— from scalding vat to kitchen table and dining room. Illustrated. 125 pages. 5x7 inches. Cloth. . . . $0.50

Harris on the Pig.

By JOSEPH HARRIS. New edition. Revised and enlarged by the author. The points of the various English and American breeds are thoroughly discussed, and the great advantage of using thoroughbred males clearly shown. The work is equally valuable to the farmer who keeps but few pigs, and to the breeder on an extensive scale. Illustrated. 318 pages. 5x7 inches. Cloth. $1.00

The Dairyman's Manual.

By HENRY STEWART, author of "The Shepherd's Manual," "Irrigation," etc. A useful and practical work, by a writer who is well known as thoroughly familiar with the subject of which he writes. Illustrated. 475 pages. 5x7 inches. Cloth. $1.50

Feeds and Feeding.

By W. A. HENRY. This handbook for students and stockmen constitutes a compendium of practical and useful knowledge on plant growth and animal nutrition, feeding stuffs, feeding animals and every detail pertaining to this important subject. It is thorough, accurate and reliable, and is the most valuable contribution to live stock literature in many years. All the latest and best information is clearly and systematically presented, making the work indispensable to every owner of live stock. 658 pages. 6x9 inches. Cloth. . . $2.00

The Propagation of Plants.

By ANDREW S. FULLER. An eminently practical and useful work describing the process of hybridizing and crossing species and varieties and also the many different modes by which cultivated plants may be propagated and multiplied. Illustrated. 350 pages. 5x7 inches. Cloth. . . $1.50

Gardening for Pleasure.

By PETER HENDERSON. A guide to the amateur in the fruit, vegetable and flower garden, with full descriptions for the greenhouse, conservatory and window garden. It meets the wants of all classes in country, city and village, who keep a garden for their own enjoyment rather than for the sale of products. Finely illustrated. 404 pages. 5x7 inches. Cloth. $1.50

Prize Gardening.

Compiled by G. Burnap Fiske. This unique book show. how to derive profit, pleasure and health from the garden, by giving the actual experiences of the successful prize winners in the American Agriculturist garden contest. Every line is from actual experience based on real work. The result is a mine and treasure house of garden practice, comprising the grand prize gardener's methods, gardening for profit, farm gardens, the home acre, town and city gardens, experimental gardening, methods under glass, success with specialties, prize flowers and fruits, gardening by women, boys and girls, irrigation, secrets, etc., etc. Illustrated from original photos. 320 pages. 5x7 inches. Cloth. $1.00

Gardening for Profit.

By Peter Henderson. The standard work on market and family gardening. The successful experience of the author for more than thirty years, and his willingness to tell, as he does in this work, the secret of his success for the benefit of others, enables him to give most valuable information. The book is profusely illustrated. 376 pages. 5x7 inches. Cloth. $1.50

The Window Flower Garden.

By Julius J. Heinrich. The author is a practical florist, and this enterprising volume embodies his personal experience in window gardening during a long period. New and enlarged edition. Illustrated. 123 pages. 5x7 inches. Cloth. $0.50

Market Gardening and Farm Notes.

By Burnett Landreth. Experiences and observation for both north and south, of interest to the amateur gardener, trucker and farmer. A novel feature of the book is the calendar of farm and garden operations for each month of the year; the chapters on fertilizers, transplanting, succession and rotation of crops, the packing, shipping and marketing of vegetables will be especially useful to market gardeners. 315 pages. 5x7 inches. Cloth. $1.00

The Study of Breeds.

By Thomas Shaw. Origin, history, distribution, characteristics, adaptability, uses, and standards of excellence of all pedigreed breeds of cattle, sheep and swine in America. The accepted text book in colleges, and the authority for farmers and breeders. Illustrated. 371 pages. 5x7 inches. Cloth. $1.50

Animal Breeding.

By Thomas Shaw. This book is the most complete and comprehensive work ever published on the subject of which it treats. It is the first book which has systematized the subject of animal breeding. The leading laws which govern this most intricate question the author has boldly defined and authoritatively arranged. The chapters which he has written on the more involved features of the subject, as sex and the relative influence of parents, should go far toward setting at rest the wildly speculative views cherished with reference to these questions. The striking originality in the treatment of the subject is no less conspicuous than the superb order and regular sequence of thought from the beginning to the end of the book. The book is intended to meet the needs of all persons interested in the breeding and rearing of live stock. Illustrated. 405 pages. 5x7 inches. Cloth. . . $1.50

Forage Crops Other Than Grasses.

By Thomas Shaw. How to cultivate, harvest and use them. Indian corn, sorghum, clover, leguminous plants, crops of the brassica genus, the cereals, millet, field roots, etc. Intensely practical and reliable. Illustrated. 287 pages. 5x7 inches. Cloth. $1.00

Soiling Crops and the Silo.

By Thomas Shaw. The growing and feeding of all kinds of soiling crops, conditions to which they are adapted, their plan in the rotation, etc. Not a line is repeated from the Forage Crops book. Best methods of building the silo, filling it and feeding ensilage. Illustrated. 364 pages. 5x7 inches. Cloth. $1.50

Stewart's Shepherd's Manual.

By Henry Stewart. A valuable practical treatise on the sheep for American farmers and sheep growers. It is so plain that a farmer or a farmer's son who has never kept a sheep may learn from its pages how to manage a flock successfully, and yet so complete that even the experienced shepherd may gather many suggestions from it. The results of personal experience of some years, with the characters of the various modern breeds of sheep, and the sheep raising capabilities of many portions of our extensive territory and that of Canada—and the careful study of the diseases to which our sheep are chiefly subject, with those by which they may eventually be afflicted through unforeseen accidents—as well as the methods of management called for under our circumstances, are carefully described. Illustrated. 276 pages. 5x7 inches. Cloth. $1.00

STANDARD BOOKS.

Pear Culture for Profit.

By P. T. QUINN, practical horticulturist. Teaching how to raise pears intelligently, and with the best results, how to find out the character of the soil, the best methods of preparing it, the best varieties to select under existing conditions, the best modes of planting, pruning, fertilizing, grafting, and utilizing the ground before the trees come into bearing, and, finally, of gathering and packing for market. Illustrated. 136 pages. 5x7 inches. Cloth. $1.00

Cranberry Culture.

By JOSEPH J. WHITE. Contents: Natural history, history of cultivation, choice of location, preparing the ground, planting the vines, management of meadows, flooding, enemies and difficulties overcome, picking, keeping, profit and loss. Illustrated. 132 pages. 5x7 inches. Cloth. . . $1.00

Ornamental Gardening for Americans.

By ELIAS A. LONG, landscape architect. A treatise on beautifying homes, rural districts and cemeteries. A plain and practical work with numerous illustrations and instructions so plain that they may be readily followed. Illustrated. 390 pages. 5x7 inches. Cloth. $1.50

Grape Culturist.

By A. S. FULLER. This is one of the very best of works on the culture of the hardy grapes, with full directions for all departments of propagation, culture, etc., with 150 excellent engravings, illustrating planting, training, grafting, etc. 282 pages. 5x7 inches. Cloth. $1.50

Gardening for Young and Old.

By JOSEPH HARRIS. A work intended to interest farmers' boys in farm gardening, which means a better and more profitable form of agriculture. The teachings are given in the familiar manner so well known in the author's "Walks and Talks on the Farm." Illustrated. 191 pages. 5x7 inches. Cloth. $1.00

Money in the Garden.

By P. T. QUINN. The author gives in a plain, practical style instructions on three distinct although closely connected branches of gardening—the kitchen garden, market garden and field culture, from successful practical experience for a term of years. Illustrated. 268 pages. 5x7 inches. Cloth. $1.00

19

www.ingramcontent.com/pod-product-compliance
Lightning Source LLC
Chambersburg PA
CBHW021409090426
42742CB00009B/1067